SKI TOURS IN LASSEN VOLCANIC NATIONAL PARK

Marcus Libkind

Bittersweet Publishing Company
Livermore, California

Cover design by Mac Smith.

Front cover photograph: Lassen Peak from Plantation Ridge by author.

Rear cover photograph by Lee Griffith.

All other photographs by author.

Edited by Clara Yen.

Library of Congress Catalog Card Number: 89-92069
International Standard Book Number: 0-931255-04-X

Published by Bittersweet Publishing Company
P.O. Box 1211, Livermore, California 94550

Printed in the United States of America

In Memory of David Gaines,

my friend

and

a friend of the earth

Contents

Introduction

On my first ski trip in Lassen Volcanic National Park, I had very mixed feelings. On the one hand I was excited to explore an area, one of our country's magnificent national parks, which was unfamiliar to me. On the other hand, I was disappointed to come to a place, filled with spectacular peaks and mountains, and find almost nothing written about the ski touring opportunities.

On that first weekend at Lassen, I grew frustrated as I explored McGowan Road only to reach road junctions, one after another, that were not shown on the USGS topographic map. Should I turn left or right, or should I stick to the straight and narrow? I felt annoyed by the continual appearance of these mystery roads, yet curious to know where they led. Finally I, in my single-mindedness, set out to explore the area and quench my curiosity.

Ski Tours in Lassen Volcanic National Park is a result of those years of exploring the park on cross-country skis. Whether you are a novice or an old timer it will introduce you to new and interesting areas which offer excellent ski touring opportunities. The information in this guidebook is useful for planning tours of an appropriate difficulty so you can enjoy pleasurable and safe touring.

The 44 tours in this book are divided into five geographical sections.

- Mineral-South of Highway 36
- Mineral-North of Highway 36
- Childs Meadows
- Southwest Entrance
- Manzanita Lake Entrance

Although you may have the tendency to skip to and begin reading the tour descriptions, I hope you will take a few minutes to read the next two sections: *Author's Note* and *How To Use This Book*. These two sections are important to your safety and understanding of how to use this guidebook.

I sincerely hope that the tours in this guidebook inspire you to explore new areas. I have thoroughly enjoyed the time spent in researching this book and I will be rewarded each time I meet another ski tourer who finds this information useful. Since I would like to hear from you, let me know your comments and suggestions.

Marcus Libkind
P.O. Box 1211
Livermore, California 94550

Author's Note

There are certain inherent dangers associated with wilderness travel in winter. No guidebook can diminish the hazards nor be a guarantee of safety. If you choose to experience the mountains in winter, you voluntarily do so knowing that there are hazards.

Although the tour descriptions make references to specific, obvious dangers, you should not assume that they are the only ones. Even the safest tour can become dangerous should you encounter poor weather, poor snow, or avalanche conditions.

Some tours may take you through private property which is not marked. If you encounter marked private property, I hope that you will respect the property rights of others so that the good reputation of ski tourers is preserved.

Although great care has gone into researching the tours in this guidebook, you may find inconsistencies due to factors such as new construction of roads and housing, policies toward plowing roads, changes in parking restrictions, and changes in trail markers. Also, extreme variations in snowfall can make a remarkable difference in how things appear. Be prepared to cope with these discrepancies should they arise.

In the final analysis, you are responsible for executing your own safe trip.

Plateau above Bumpass Hell

How To Use This Book

The short time it takes you to read this section will increase the usefulness of this guidebook. Each tour description in this guidebook contains a summary, an introduction, and a mileage log. The summary box gives you at a glance the significant characteristics of the tour. The introduction describes the aesthetic features of the tour, special considerations, alternate routes, and general information which will be helpful in planning a tour. The mileage log describes the route in an easy to follow format.

Summary Box

Difficulty: The difficulty ratings are based on four criteria: length, elevation change, steepness, and navigation. A 5 level scale for rating the overall difficulty of the tours is used. The skills associated with each level are:

1 — Beginner

- Little or no previous ski touring experience
- Ability to follow simple directions without map or compass

2 — Advanced beginner

- Proficiency in the basic techniques: diagonal stride, side-step, kick turn, step turn, snowplow, and snowplow turn
- Ability to control speed on gradual downhills
- Ability to negotiate short, moderately steep sections of terrain
- Ability to follow simple directions in conjunction with a map

3 — Intermediate

- Excellent proficiency in all the basic techniques plus the traverse and herringbone on moderately steep terrain
- Ability to negotiate long, moderately steep, and short, steep sections of terrain
- Good stamina
- Ability to navigate using a topographic map
- Ability to use a compass to determine general orientation

4 — Advanced intermediate

> • Excellent proficiency in all ski touring techniques
> • Ability to negotiate long, steep sections of terrain including densely wooded areas
> • Strong skier
> • Ability to navigate using a topographic map and compass

5 — Expert

> • Excellent all around ski tourer and mountain person
> • Ability to negotiate very steep terrain
> • Exceptional endurance
> • Ability to navigate using a topographic map and compass

Two tours may be assigned the same rating but vary greatly in the skills required. For example, both a tour on a road which is long and a tour which is short but requires navigation by map and compass may be rated 3. For this reason the difficulty ratings should only be used as a general guide for selecting a tour of appropriate difficulty. Check the summary box for information regarding length, elevation, and navigation to determine whether your abilities match the demands of a tour. Also, refer to the introduction which describes the tour route for special considerations.

The tours were rated assuming ideal snow conditions. Deep powder will make travel slower and more difficult. Ice will make all tours much more difficult. If you are faced with icy conditions in the morning, you might consider waiting until early afternoon to begin, when hopefully, the snow will have thawed.

Length: The length is an estimate of the horizontal mileage as obtained from the topographic maps. Whether the mileage is one-way or round trip is also noted.

In the Southwest Entrance section, I describe four "cutoff" tours which bypass sections of the standard tour along Lassen Park Road. The mileage given is measured from the point where the cutoff leaves the road to the point where the cutoff intersects the road again. Following the mileage number, the distance that is saved is in parentheses. Also, several tours begin on snow-covered Lassen Park Road and you must add the mileage required to reach the starting point.

Elevation: The first number is the elevation at the starting point of the tour in feet above sea level. The elevation is a major consideration when planning tours early or late in the season.

The elevation at the starting point is followed by a slash and the elevation change for the entire tour. The change is written as "+gain, –loss." "Nil" is used where the change is negligible.

10

Navigation: The navigational difficulty of each tour is based on untracked snow and good visibility. The key words and phrases are:

Adjacent to plowed road — Tour is located almost completely within sight of a plowed road.

Road — Tour follows snow-covered roads. Although roads are normally easy to follow, a small road or a road in open terrain may be difficult to locate or follow.

Marked trail — Tour follows marked trail; may require basic map-reading skills. Markers are normally brightly

Brokeoff Mountain

colored pieces of metal attached to trees well above the snow level or strips of brightly colored ribbon attached to tree branches close to the trail. Blazes which mark summer trails are not considered markers since they are often obscured by snow. Whenever you are on a marked trail, you must pay careful attention to locating each successive marker which may not be ideally placed. Even with a marked trail, you will probably need some knowledge of the route and basic map-reading skills to follow it.

Map — Tour requires the ability to read a topographic map since the tour follows well-defined terrain such as creeks, valleys, and ridges. Also remember that poor visibility can make route-finding impossible without a compass and expert knowledge of its use.

Compass — Tour requires the use of a compass in conjunction with a topographic map. In some instances the compass is mainly for safety, but other routes require you to follow compass bearings.

Time: To give you a general idea of the length of time required to complete a tour, the following key words and phrases are used:

- Short
- Few hours
- Half day
- Most of a day
- Full day
- Very long day
- Few days

Some of the factors which will affect your trip time include snow and weather conditions, your skiing ability and physical strength, characteristics of the tour, and your personal habits. When I made the estimates, I also considered periods for reasonable rests and for route-finding.

Always keep in mind that the days are short in the mid-winter months. Very long tours are best done in early spring when the days are longer.

Start and end: Described are detailed directions for locating the starting and ending points of the tour. The ending point is omitted if the tour route returns to where it began. It is your responsibility to determine whether it is legal to park at these points.

Several tours begin on highways where wide shoulder areas exist for parking, not plowed trailheads. At the time this book was published, cars were not ticketed as long as they were completely off the highway and there was no need for plowing. You should check with local authorities for any recent policy changes.

Mileage Log

The mileage log is designed to make it easy for readers to follow the route description and keep track of their progress. Keep in mind that the description is not a substitute for knowledge, skill, and common sense. The following sample mileage log entry will help you understand how to read the log entries.

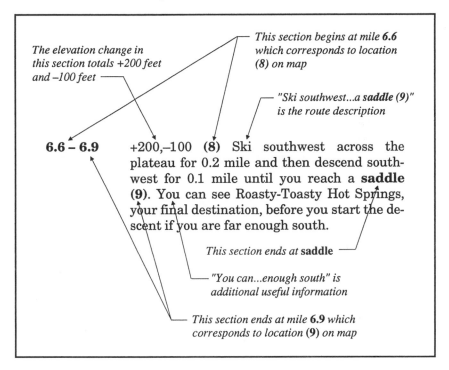

Maps

Most tours require that you have and are able to read a topographic map. Parts of United States Geological Survey (USGS) maps are reproduced in this guidebook; the map reproduction number and its page location are at the beginning of each tour adjacent to the tour name.

Except for a few tours south of Highway 36 near Mineral, all the tours can be found on the USGS Lassen Volcanic National Park and Vicinity special map. For the tours south of Highway 36 you will need a Lassen Peak 15′ series map. The following diagram shows the relationship between the large special map and the individual 15′ series maps.

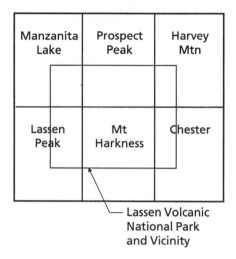

| Manzanita Lake | Prospect Peak | Harvey Mtn |
| Lassen Peak | Mt Harkness | Chester |

Lassen Volcanic National Park and Vicinity

United States Geological Survey maps are available at most mountain shops, at the USGS offices in Menlo Park, CA and San Francisco, CA, and by mail from:

United States Geological Survey
Box 25286 Denver Federal Building
Denver, Colorado 80225

Wilderness Press publishes a revised (updated) version of the Lassen Volcanic National Park and Vicinity special map which also includes an index and other information. It is available at most mountain shops or from Wilderness Press at:

Wilderness Press
2440 Bancroft Way
Berkeley, California 94704

Topographic Map Legend

5　　　Landmark number (corresponds to mileage log)

━ ━　　Ski route

→　　　Known avalanche path

Be aware that almost any slope can become an avalanche hazard should the right snow and weather conditions arise. Inquire at the nearest Forest Service or Park Service office if you have any doubts about the safety of your route.

Mineral - South of Highway 36

South of Highway 36 between Mineral and Morgan Summit there are a number of roads which can be linked into excellent one-way and loop ski tours. Do not rule this area out because of the Morgan Summit Snowmobile Park; there are times when you can ski in this area and never see a single snowmobile — especially on a weekday.

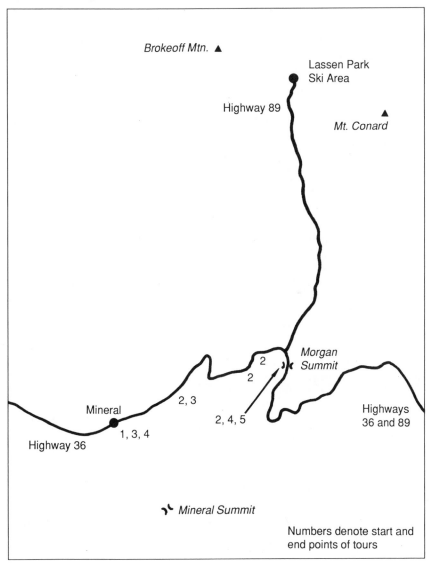

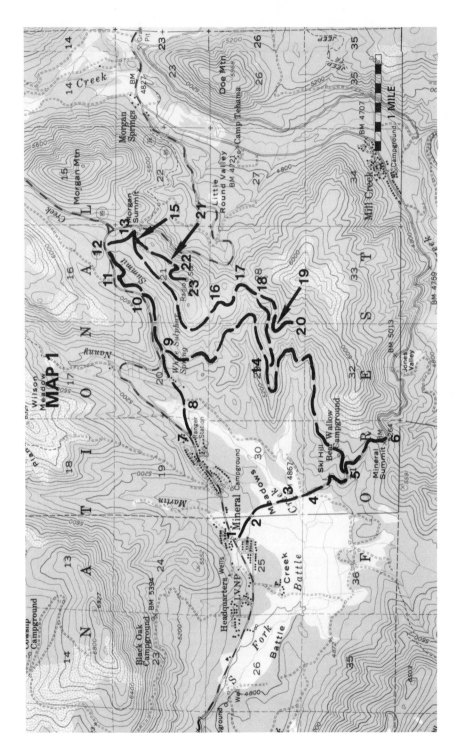

MAP 1
PAGE 16

Mineral to Mineral Summit

Difficulty	1 for first 1.5 miles and 2 for next 0.6 mile
Length	4 miles round trip
Elevation	4900/+350,–350 round trip
Navigation	Road
Time	Few hours
Start	The junction of Highway 172 (Mill Creek Road) and Highway 36 in the center of Mineral. The tour begins on Highway 172 just south of the gas station.

The Mineral to Mineral Summit tour is absolutely flat for the first 0.9 mile as it follows snow-covered Highway 172 across Battle Creek Meadows. In the late afternoon following a snowfall, one tends to linger in the beautiful meadows as the sun sets. You should be aware, however, that the meadows are privately owned, and the fence means do not trespass.

Past the meadows the road climbs moderately for 1.2 miles to Mineral Summit where the woods obscure all views. The road beyond the summit is described in the Mill Creek to Mineral Summit tour (no. 18). The return run from the summit to the meadow is great fun when the snow conditions are good.

Mileage Log

0.0 – 0.2 +0 (1) Ski southeast on Highway 172 for 0.2 mile until you reach **Martin Creek (2)**.

0.2 – 0.7 +0 (2) Ski south on Highway 172 for 0.5 mile until you reach **Battle Creek (3)**.

0.7 – 0.9 +0 (3) Ski south on Highway 172 for 0.2 mile until you reach the **edge of Battle Creek Meadows (4)**.

0.9 – 1.5 +100 (4) Ski south on Highway 172 for 0.6 mile until you reach a **road junction (5)**. The fork on the north (left) is part of the Conard Grove to Mineral tour (no. 3) and the Morgan Summit to Mineral tour (no. 4). The Mineral Summit tour continues on Highway 172 (straight).

1.5 – 2.1 +250 (5) Ski south (straight) on Highway 172 for 0.6 mile until you reach **Mineral Summit (6)**.

2 Conard Grove to Morgan Summit

MAP 1
PAGE 16

Difficulty	1 – 3
Length	Up to 3 miles one-way
Elevation	5000/Up to +700 or −700 one-way
Navigation	Road or road and map
Time	Short to half day
Start-End	There are four possible starting and ending points for this tour.

1. The south side of Highway 36 at the junction of Highway 36 and the west end of snow-covered Conard Grove, 1.1 miles east of the Mineral Post Office and 0.1 mile east of the ranger station.

2. The south side of Highway 36 at the junction of Highway 36 and the east end of snow-covered Conard Grove, 3.4 miles east of the Mineral Post Office. There is a turnout on the south side of the highway.

3. The south side of Highway 36 at the Christie Hill Road Trailhead, 3.7 miles east of the Mineral Post Office.

4. The Snowmobile Park at Morgan Summit. The park is located on the west (south) side of Highway 89, 0.2 mile south (east) of the junction of Highways 36 and 89. The tour begins or ends on the snow-covered road located on the west side of the parking area.

The perfect day to enjoy the Conard Grove to Morgan Summit tour is during or immediately after a snowfall. With fresh snow the decent is fast, but not uncontrollably so. The tour is also very sheltered, except for the first 0.5 mile, which makes it a good choice for stormy weather.

There are three distinct sections between the ranger station and Morgan Summit from which skiers of all abilities can choose. There is a 0.5 mile flat section on Conard Grove, a 1.1 mile climb on Conard Grove, and a final 1.1 mile climb to Morgan Summit.

Although you can start this tour from either end, the description begins near the ranger station and climbs to Morgan Summit. Most skiers will probably ski in one direction and retrace their tracks on the return trip. If you have a shuttle, you can do an all downhill tour in the opposite direction.

2

Mileage Log

0.0 – 0.3 +0 **(7)** Ski east on Conard Grove for 0.3 mile until you reach the **bridge (8)** across Nancy Creek.

0.3 – 1.0 +250 **(8)** Ski east on Conard Grove for 0.7 mile until you reach a **road junction (9)**. The road to the south (right) which crosses Summit Creek leads to Highway 172 and Mineral, and is described in the Conard Grove to Mineral tour (no. 3).

1.0 – 1.6 +200 **(9)** Ski east (straight) on Conard Grove for 0.6 mile until you reach **Highway 36 (10)** at a turnout.

1.6 – 1.9 +100 **(10)** Ski north and parallel to the highway for 0.3 mile until you reach the **Christie Hill Road Trailhead (11)**. It may be difficult to see the trailhead which is on the north side of the highway, but there is a sign on the south side of the highway which reads "Lassen Volcanic National Park – Left turn ½ mile."

1.9 – 2.3 +50 **(11)** Ski south (away) from the highway for 100 yards until you find an obvious break in the brush; turn northeast (left) and ski through the brush and parallel to the highway on a logging road for 0.4 mile until you reach **Summit Creek (12)**.

2.3 – 2.7 +100 **(12)** Ski southeast for 0.4 mile until you reach the **Snowmobile Park (13)** at Morgan Summit.

3   Conard Grove to Mineral

MAP 1
PAGE 16

Difficulty	2
Length	7 miles one-way
Elevation	5000/+350,−450 one-way
Navigation	Road
Time	Half day
Start	South side of Highway 36 at the junction of Highway 36 and the west end of snow-covered Conard Grove, 1.1 miles east of the Mineral Post Office and 0.1 mile east of the ranger station.
End	The junction Highway 172 (Mill Creek Road) and Highway 36 in the center of Mineral. The tour ends on Highway 172 just south of the gas station.

The Conard Grove to Mineral tour is nice because there is enough variation to keep this easy-to-follow route on roads interesting. The shuttle for this one-way tour is short enough that you might want to consider walking it, and the thought of hot toddies waiting at the end makes even the worst weather on this tour seem tolerable.

Mileage Log

0.0 – 0.3   +0 **(7)** Ski east on Conard Grove for 0.3 mile until you reach the **bridge (8)** across Nancy Creek.

0.3 – 1.0   +250 **(8)** Ski east on Conard Grove for 0.7 mile until you reach a **road junction (9)**. The Conard Grove to Morgan Summit tour (no. 2) continues straight ahead while this tour turns south (right) and crosses Summit Creek.

1.0 – 2.9   +100 **(9)** Ski south (right) on the snow-covered road for 1.9 miles until you reach a **road junction (14)**. The road to the south (left) is part of the Morgan Summit to Mineral tour (no. 4) and this tour continues straight ahead.

2.9 – 5.6   −350 **(14)** Zig-zag southwest (straight) on the snow-covered road for 2.7 miles until you reach snow-covered **Highway 172 (5)**. Mineral Summit and Mill Creek are to the southeast (left) and Mineral is to the north (right).

5.6 – 7.1   −100 **(5)** Ski north (right) on Highway 172 for 1.5 miles until you reach **Highway 36 and Mineral (1)**.

Fresh snow on road south of Highway 36

MAP 1
PAGE 16

4 Morgan Summit to Mineral

Difficulty	3
Length	7 miles one-way
Elevation	5700/–800 one-way
Navigation	Road
Time	Most of a day
Start	Snowmobile Park at Morgan Summit. The park is located on the west (south) side of Highway 89, 0.2 mile south (east) of the junction of Highways 36 and 89. The tour begins on the snow-covered road located on the west side of the parking area.
End	The junction Highway 172 (Mill Creek Road) and Highway 36 in the center of Mineral. The tour ends on Highway 172 just south of the gas station.

From Morgan Summit this tour winds around canyons and along hillsides before finally descending to Battle Creek Meadows and Mineral. Along the route you will have an opportunity to make a side trip (1.4 miles round trip) to a grand view of Battle Creek Meadows. Combined with the side trip, this tour is the longest tour in the Mineral area south of Highway 36 and will keep most skiers busy for most of a day.

Be aware that this road is one of the most popular snowmobiling routes in the area. However, on many occasions it makes an excellent tour.

Mileage Log

0.0 – 0.0 +0 **(13)** Ski west on the snow-covered road for 50 yards until you reach a **road junction (15)**. The south (left) fork is part of the Relay Station tour (no. 5) and this tour continues on the north (right) fork.

0.0 – 1.7 –50 **(15)** Ski generally southwest on the snow-covered road for 1.7 miles until you reach a **road junction (16)**. The east (left) fork leads to a saddle and this tour continues on the west (right) fork. In this section you will have views down into Summit Creek and west to the cliffs above Mineral which are the destination of the Battle Creek Overlook tour (no. 14).

1.7 – 2.1 –50 **(16)** Ski generally south (right) on the snow-covered road for 0.4 mile until you reach a **saddle (17)**.

At 0.1 mile you will pass a road on your right. Just before the saddle you will pass under powerlines, immediately after the powerlines you will pass a road on your left, and at the saddle you will find a fork in the road.

2.1 – 2.3 +0 **(17)** Take the west (right) fork and follow it for 0.2 mile until you reach a **road junction (18)**. The east (left) fork leads to a viewpoint and is described below. This tour continues on the west (right) fork.

2.3 – 3.2 –250 **(18)** Descend the west (right) fork for 0.9 mile until you reach a **road junction (14)**. The continuous gradient on this narrow descent can make this section difficult. The road you intersect is part of the Conard Grove to Mineral tour (no. 3).

3.2 – 5.9 –350 **(14)** Turn west (left) and zig-zag southwest on the snow-covered road for 2.7 miles until you reach snow-covered **Highway 172 (5)**. Mineral Summit and Mill Creek are to the southeast (left) and Mineral is to the north (right).

5.6 – 7.1 –100 **(5)** Ski north (right) on Highway 172 for 1.5 miles until you reach **Highway 36 and Mineral (1)**.

The following is a description of the side trip which begins at junction (18) and leads to the view of Battle Creek Meadows.

2.3 – 2.8 +0 **(18)** Ski southwest on the east (left) fork for 0.5 mile until you reach a **point (19)**.

2.8 – 3.0 +0 **(19)** Ski south on the snow-covered road for 0.2 mile until you reach the **view (20)** to the west (right) of Battle Creek Meadows.

5 Relay Station

MAP 1
PAGE 16

Difficulty	3
Length	3 miles round trip
Elevation	5700/+400,−400 round trip
Navigation	Road
Time	Short
Start	Snowmobile Park at Morgan Summit. The park is located on the west (south) side of Highway 89, 0.2 mile south (east) of the junction of Highways 36 and 89. The tour begins on the snow-covered road located on the west side of the parking area.

It is a short, steady climb on a road through thick woods to the relay station atop a small knoll. Although the trees on the summit block the view, halfway up there are excellent views of Morgan Valley and the snowcapped peaks of Lassen Park. The return run is a brisk, continuous glide requiring speed control in the confines of the road.

This tour would be popular if it were located anywhere else. Unfortunately, it is located in an area which is specifically designated for snowmobilers. Therefore, the best times for this tour are mid-week and immediately after a fresh snowfall. For an interesting change of pace, get up early following a snowfall and do this tour before breakfast. You will beat the snowmobilers, have great snow, and those buckwheat pancakes will taste better than ever.

Mileage Log

0.0 – 0.0   +0 **(13)** Ski west on the snow-covered road for 50 yards until you reach a **road junction (15)**. The north (right) fork is part of the Morgan Summit to Mineral tour (no. 4) and this tour follows the lesser south (left) fork.

0.0 – 0.5   +250 **(15)** Ski southwest on the south (left) fork for 0.5 mile until you reach a point where the **road levels off (21)**. A short ski off the road to the east (left) from where the road levels will lead to a view of Morgan Valley.

0.5 – 0.6   +0 **(21)** Ski southwest on the snow-covered road for 0.1 mile until you reach a **sharp turn (22)** to the north (right). Immediately after making the turn take time to enjoy the view north toward the Southwest Entrance to Lassen Volcanic National Park. The three most prominent peaks are Brokeoff Mountain, Lassen Peak and Mt. Conard.

0.6 – 0.9   +150 **(22)** Make a loop north and then south on the snow-covered road for 0.3 mile until you reach the **relay station (23)**.

Battle Creek Meadows

McGowan Road

Mineral - North of Highway 36

North of Mineral and Highway 36, south of Lassen Volcanic National Park, east of Viola Road, and west of Highway 89 lies a 25 square mile piece of land which offers excellent ski touring opportunities. Beginner and intermediate skiers will find a better selection of tours in this area than in the park itself, although it can not match the beauty of the park.

Here you will find Nancy Creek Road, Christie Hill Road, and McGowan Road which are designated for ski touring only. Combine these with the other snow-covered roads in the area to create an assortment of one-way and loop tours.

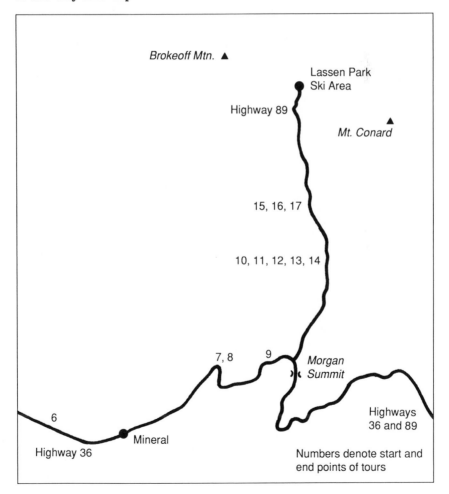

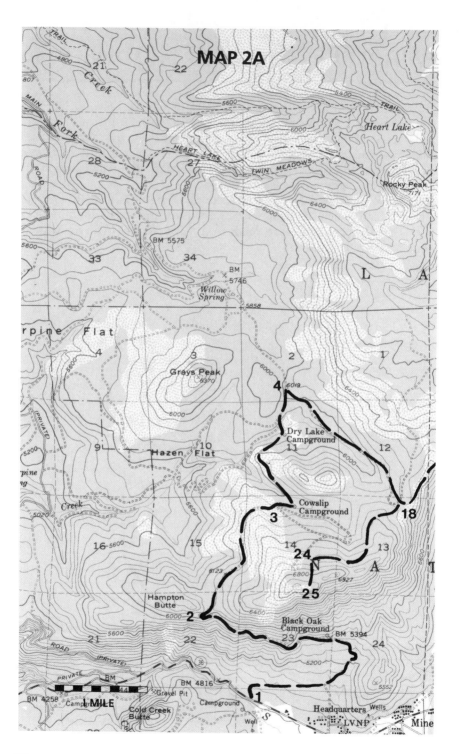

MAP 2A

28

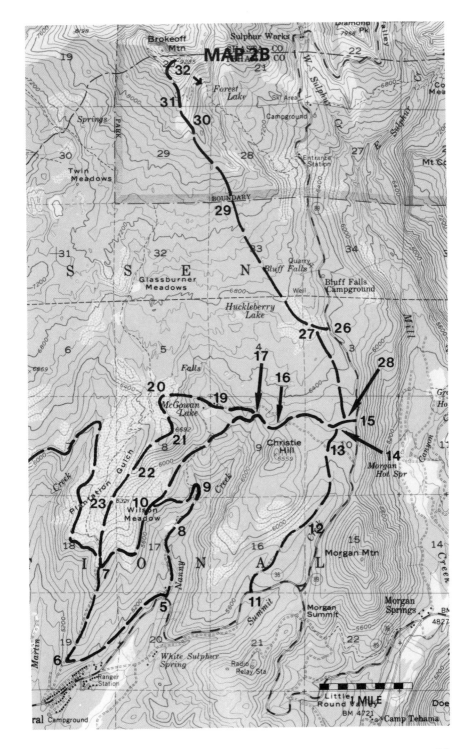

6 Viola Road

Difficulty	3
Length	6 miles one-way to McGowan Road
Elevation	4800/+1350,–150 one-way to McGowan Road
Navigation	Road
Time	Half day one-way to McGowan Road
Start	The north side of Highway 36 at Viola Road, 1.0 mile west of Lassen Volcanic National Park Headquarters in Mineral. The actual starting point is 100 yards up Viola Road at the Mineral disposal site.
End	Junction of Viola Road and McGowan Road. There is no vehicle access to this point. Return via the same route or one of the other routes described in this section.

There are two good reasons you may want to ski on Viola Road. First, combined with McGowan Road it makes a 15.6-mile one-way tour completely on roads with no retracing. Second, it is the shortest route to Battle Creek Overlook (no. 14).

There are also two reasons why you may not want to ski on Viola Road. First, the first three miles are a steep, continuous grind with no particular rewards unless you enjoy a very fast descent on a road. Second, it is frequented by snowmobiles.

Mileage Log

0.0 – 3.3 +1200 **(1)** Loop north on Viola Road for 3.3 miles until you reach a **sharp turn (2)**. A half mile before reaching the turn you will have a view of Battle Creek Meadows and at the turn you will have a view west toward the Upper Sacramento Valley.

3.3 – 4.9 +150,–50 **(2)** Ski north on Viola Road for 1.6 miles until you reach a **road junction (3)**. The road on the southeast (right) side of Viola Road marks the location where you leave Viola Road to ascend to Battle Creek Lookout as described below.

4.9 – 6.4 –100 **(3)** Ski north on Viola Road for 1.5 miles until you reach **McGowan Road (4)**. In this section you will pass several logging roads, and 0.3 mile after you pass Dry Lake you will reach McGowan Road (no. 10).

6

To reach Battle Creek Overlook

At junction (3) there is a major road to the southeast (right) (29N81). Locate the lesser road located 25 feet to the south of the major road. Start on the lesser road and climb south for one mile until you reach the ridge top and the view of Battle Creek Meadows below. In this one mile you will probably see several logging roads. Only follow them if they head in the correct direction. The slope you ascend makes a wonderful descent when the conditions are good.

Plantation Ridge

7 Old Brokeoff Trail

Difficulty	3 (4 in the reverse direction)
Length	2 miles one-way to McGowan Road
Elevation	5100/+750 one-way to McGowan Road
Navigation	Road
Time	Short one-way
Start	Nancy Creek Road Trailhead on Highway 36, 2.0 miles east of the Mineral Post Office and 2.3 miles west of the junction of Highways 36 and 89.
End	Junction of Old Brokeoff Trail and McGowan Road. There is no vehicle access to this point. Return via the same route or one of the other routes described in this section.

Old Brokeoff Trail has a character different from all the other roads in the Mineral area — it is short, steep, narrow, and a challenge to descend. Many skiers will choose to ski it in the uphill direction, and link it with McGowan Road (no. 10) and Nancy Creek Road (no. 8) to make a one-way loop. However, if you choose to enjoy the thrill of the descent, pick a day when there is plenty of snow and the snow conditions are favorable.

Mileage Log

0.0 – 1.3 +150 **(5)** At the trailhead locate the road that leads southwest (left); do not confuse it with Nancy Creek Road. Follow the snow-covered road southwest for 1.3 miles until you reach a **road junction (6)** at a broad ridge. This junction is not obvious. The main road turns north (right) here and there are minor roads on both the northeast (right) and southwest (left) sides. Old Brokeoff Trail actually begins here on the northeast side of the main road.

1.3 – 2.4 +600 **(6)** Turn northeast (right) onto Old Brokeoff Trail and climb for 1.1 miles until you reach **McGowan Road (7)**.

Nancy Creek Road **8**

Difficulty	1 – 2
Length	2 miles one-way to McGowan Road
Elevation	5100/+650 one-way to McGowan Road
Navigation	Road
Time	Short one-way
Start	Nancy Creek Road Trailhead on Highway 36, 2.0 miles east of the Mineral Post Office and 2.3 miles west of the junction of Highways 36 and 89.
End	Junction of Nancy Creek Road and McGowan Road. There is no vehicle access to this point. Return via the same route or one of the other routes described in this section.

Nancy Creek Road makes an excellent tour by itself but you can combine it with other roads in the area to form a tailor-made loop and/or one-way tour. For example, without retracing your tracks and without a shuttle car you can create a tour by combining the Old Brokeoff Trail tour (no. 7), the McGowan Road tour (no. 10), and this tour into a loop.

The Nancy Creek Road tour is popular because it is one of three roads in the area designated as Nordic trails and is closed to snowmobiles. The other two are Christie Hill Road (no. 9) and McGowan Road (no.10).

Mileage Log

0.0 – 0.8   +250 **(5)** Ski north on Nancy Creek Road for 0.8 mile until you reach small **Wilson Meadow (8)**.

0.8 – 1.4   +150 **(8)** Ski north on Nancy Creek Road for 0.6 mile until you reach a **180 degree turn (9)**.

1.4 – 2.1   +250 **(9)** Ski southwest and west on Nancy Creek Road for 0.7 mile until you reach **McGowan Road (10)**.

Lassen Peak

Christie Hill Road 9

Difficulty	1 – 2
Length	2 miles one-way to McGowan Road
Elevation	5550/+650 one-way to McGowan Road
Navigation	Road
Time	Short one-way
Start	Christie Hill Road Trailhead on Highway 36, 3.7 miles east of the Mineral Post Office and 0.6 mile west of the junction of Highways 36 and 89.
End	Junction of Christie Hill Road and McGowan Road. There is no vehicle access to this point. Return via the same route or one of the other routes described in this section.

Christie Hill Road, which has been set aside as a Nordic trail and is closed to snowmobiles, is a popular starting point. However, unless you return via the same route you will need a shuttle car. You can create an excellent one-way tour by linking the Christie Hill tour with the McGowan Road tour (no. 10) and the Nancy Creek Road tour (no. 8) for a net elevation loss of 450 feet.

Mileage Log

0.0 – 1.0   +250 **(11)** Ski northeast on Christie Hill Road for 1.0 mile until you reach the **building (12)** located on the east (right) side of the road. Don't be surprised if you pass by the building without noticing it.

1.0 – 1.9   +300 **(12)** Ski northeast on Christie Hill Road for 0.9 mile until you reach a **road junction (13)**. The terrain at the junction is fairly level and open, and sometimes it is difficult to tell that you are at a Y intersection. This tour continues on the east (right) fork.

1.9 – 2.1   +100 **(13)** Ski north on the east (right) fork for 0.2 mile until you reach **McGowan Road (14)**.

10 McGowan Road

MAPS 2A-2B
PAGES 28-29

Difficulty	1 – 3
Length	9 miles one-way to Viola Road
Elevation	6200/+500, −700 one-way to Viola Road
Navigation	Road
Time	Half day one-way
Start	McGowan Road Trailhead on Highway 89, 2.0 miles north of the junction of Highways 36 and 89, and 3.5 miles south of the Lassen Park Ski Area. There is a turnout, parking space, and the trailhead on the west side of the highway.
End	Junction of McGowan Road and Viola Road. There is no vehicle access to this point. Return via the same route or one of the other routes described in this section.

Except for the Southwest Entrance to the park itself, there is good reason for the McGowan Road Trailhead being the most popular starting point for cross-country skiers in the Lassen area. McGowan Road is the main access route into an area which has good terrain for touring and is one of the roads in the area designated as a Nordic trail where snowmobiles are prohibited. From the road you can branch off in a number of directions, and the roads in this area can be linked to create interesting loop and one-way tours.

Mileage Log

0.0 – 0.2   +0 **(15)** Ski west on McGowan Road for 0.2 mile until you reach the junction with **Christie Hill Road (14)** (no. 9) which is on the south (left) side of McGowan Road.

0.2 – 1.0   +0 **(14)** Ski west (straight) on McGowan Road for 0.8 mile until you reach the location where the **road begins to descend (16)**. Beyond this point McGowan Road drops steadily for 1.9 miles and for beginners may be difficult when icy.

1.0 – 1.3   −50 **(16)** Ski west on McGowan Road for 0.3 mile until you reach the **McGowan Lake turnoff (17)** which is on the north (right) side of McGowan Road. The turnoff to McGowan Lake is easily missed if you are skiing fast.

36

1.3 – 2.9   −400 **(17)** Ski southwest (straight) on McGowan Road for 1.6 miles until you reach the junction with **Nancy Creek Road (10)** (no. 8) which is on the southeast (left) side of McGowan Road.

2.9 – 4.0   +100 **(10)** Ski southwest (straight) on McGowan Road for 1.1 miles until you reach a **road junction (7)**. At the junction the fairly obvious road on the north (right) side of McGowan Road is part of the Plantation Ridge tour (no. 13), and the McGowan Lake and Plantation Ridge Loop tour (no. 12). Twenty-five yards past the obvious road is an obscure road on the south (left) side of McGowan Road. This road is Old Brokeoff Trail (no. 7).

4.0 – 7.5   +400 **(7)** Ski north and then west (straight) on McGowan Road for 3.5 miles until you reach a **road junction (18)**. The major road on the north (right) side of McGowan Road is not especially interesting. The lesser road on the south (left) side of McGowan Road is part of the Battle Creek Overlook tour (no. 14).

7.5 – 9.2   −250 **(18)** Ski northwest (straight) on McGowan Road for 1.7 miles until you reach **Viola Road (4)** (no. 6).

11 McGowan Lake

Difficulty	2
Length	4 miles round trip
Elevation	6200/+250,–250 round trip
Navigation	Road
Time	Few hours
Start	McGowan Road Trailhead on Highway 89, 2.0 miles north of the junction of Highways 36 and 89, and 3.5 miles south of the Lassen Park Ski Area. There is a turnout, parking space, and the trailhead on the west side of the highway.

McGowan Lake is an excellent destination for skiers who want to get off the main ski trail in this area. The lake is situated in a bowl and affords a pleasant setting in which to relax, eat lunch, and enjoy the sunshine. The tour to the lake is also the beginning of the longer McGowan Lake and Plantation Ridge tour (no. 12).

McGowan Lake is situated on private property and although ski tourers have used the lake as a destination in the past the owners have the right to restrict entry. Please stay away from the cabin and abide by all posted notices.

Mileage Log

0.0 – 1.3   –50 **(15)** Ski west on McGowan Road for 1.3 miles until you reach the **McGowan Lake turnoff (17)** which is on the north (right) side of McGowan Road. It is easy to miss the turnoff if you are skiing fast. Refer to the McGowan Road tour (no. 10) for additional information about this section.

1.3 – 1.8   +50,–150 **(17)** Turn north (right) and ski west on McGowan Lake Road for 0.5 mile until you reach **McGowan Lake (19)**.

Brokeoff Mountain

12 McGowan Lake and Plantation Ridge Loop

Difficulty	4
Length	9 miles round trip
Elevation	6200/+1250,−1250 round trip
Navigation	Road and map
Time	Full day
Start	McGowan Road Trailhead on Highway 89, 2.0 miles north of the junction of Highways 36 and 89, and 3.5 miles south of the Lassen Park Ski Area. There is a turnout, parking space, and the trailhead on the west side of the highway.

If there is one tour in the McGowan Road area that stands out among all others, it is the McGowan Lake and Plantation Ridge Loop. Of the entire nine miles, the route only retraces itself for one mile. In addition to easy skiing along roads, a steep climb will take you to the top of a ridge which offers a magnificent panorama including Brokeoff Mountain, Lassen Peak, and Mt. Conard.

The route off the ridge is a two-mile run along its crest; most of the time the skiing is easy, but in a few places the skiing is tricky. Plantation Ridge also affords excellent downhill runs into Plantation Gulch.

The Plantation Ridge tour (no. 13) describes an alternate tour along the ridge which avoids the very steep climb from McGowan Lake.

Mileage Log

0.0 – 1.3 −50 **(15)** Ski west on McGowan Road for 1.3 miles until you reach the **McGowan Lake turnoff (17)** which is on the north (right) side of McGowan Road. The turnoff is easy to miss if you are skiing fast. Refer to the McGowan Road tour (no. 10) for additional information about this section.

1.3 – 1.8 +50,−150 **(17)** Turn north (right) and ski west on McGowan Lake Road for 0.5 mile until you reach **McGowan Lake (19)**. Refer to the McGowan Lake tour (no. 11) for information about the private property in this area.

1.8 – 2.5 +500 **(19)** Climb west for 0.7 mile until you reach the **low point on the ridge (20)** which is north of Peak 6692. This very steep climb is through trees.

2.5 – 2.9   +150 **(20)** Ski southeast along the ridge for 0.4 mile until you reach **Peak 6692 (21)**.

2.9 – 3.4   +50,–250 **(21)** Ski southwest along the ridge for 0.5 mile until you reach a **high point (22)**. Part of the ridge is very narrow and the skiing is easiest along its west (right) side where the terrain is open.

3.4 – 3.9   +50,–250 **(22)** Ski southwest along the ridge for 0.5 mile until you reach **Peak 6321 (23)**. When snow conditions permit, from just north of Peak 6321 you can descend east (left) for 0.4 mile until you reach the McGowan Road and Nancy Creek Road junction (10). This alternate route reduces the length of the tour by 1.5 miles.

3.9 – 4.6   –450 **(23)** Ski south along the broad ridge and jeep road for 0.7 mile until you reach **McGowan Road (7)**. In this section you first descend the broad ridge for 0.3 mile until it splits. Then you follow the east (left) fork of the ridge for 0.1 mile through brush until you reach a jeep road. Finally you follow the jeep road south for 0.3 mile until you reach McGowan Road.

4.6 – 5.7   –100 **(7)** Ski northeast (left) on McGowan Road for 1.1 miles until you reach the junction with **Nancy Creek Road (10)**.

5.7 – 7.3   +400 **(10)** Ski northeast (straight) on McGowan Road for 1.6 miles until you reach the **McGowan Lake turn-off (17)**.

7.3 – 8.6   +50 **(17)** Ski east (straight) on McGowan Road for 1.3 miles until you reach the **McGowan Road Trailhead (15)**.

13 Plantation Ridge

Difficulty	3
Length	Up to 6 miles one-way to Peak 6692
Elevation	6200/Up to +1050,−550 one-way to Peak 6692
Navigation	Road and map
Time	Up to full day
Start	McGowan Road Trailhead on Highway 89, 2.0 miles north of the junction of Highways 36 and 89, and 3.5 miles south of the Lassen Park Ski Area. There is a turnout, parking space, and the trailhead on the west side of the highway.

This is probably the most interesting intermediate tour in the area. It combines easy skiing along roads with a delightful climb along a ridge. For most of the distance the ridge is broad, however, in a few places the ridge is narrow and the skiing is tricky.

The ridge and its high points offer many fine vistas which include Brokeoff Mountain, Lassen Peak, and Mt. Conard. Of course, the highlight for you may be the return descent along the ridge. You may also want to enjoy practicing your downhill techniques on the slopes which descend into Plantation Gulch.

Advanced-intermediate skiers may want to consider a variation of this tour — the McGowan Lake and Plantation Ridge Loop tour (no. 12).

Mileage Log

0.0 – 4.0   +100,−450 **(15)** Ski west and southwest on McGowan Road for 4.0 miles until you reach a **road junction (7)**. There will be a fairly obvious road on the north (right) side of McGowan Road. Refer to the McGowan Road tour (no. 10) for information about the other road junctions in this section.

4.0 – 4.7   +450 **(7)** Turn off McGowan Road and ski north (right) on the road and broad ridge for 0.7 mile until you reach **Peak 6321 (23)**. In this section you will first follow the road for 0.3 mile. Then you will leave the road (there is no landmark) and follow the broad ridge for 0.4 mile until you reach Peak 6321.

4.7 – 5.2   +250,−50 **(23)** Ski northeast along the ridge for 0.5 mile until you reach a **high point (22)**.

5.2 – 5.7   +250,–50 **(22)** Ski northeast along the ridge for 0.5 mile until you reach **Peak 6692 (21)**. Because part of the ridge is very narrow, the skiing is easiest along the open terrain of its west (left) side.

Cornices on Brokeoff Mountain

14   Battle Creek Overlook

Difficulty	4
Length	18 miles round trip
Elevation	6200/+1600,−1600 round trip
Navigation	Road and map
Time	Very long day
Start	McGowan Road Trailhead on Highway 89, 2.0 miles north of the junction of Highways 36 and 89, and 3.5 miles south of the Lassen Park Ski Area. There is a turnout, parking space, and the trailhead on the west side of the highway.

Ski to Battle Creek Overlook to treat yourself to a bird's-eye view of Battle Creek Meadows. Although the route to the overlook via Viola Road (no. 6) is shorter, this route via McGowan Road is technically easier. Except for the last 0.3 mile it is entirely along snow-covered roads.

You can make a very interesting 15-mile, one-way tour by skiing to Battle Creek Overlook via this route, then descending to Viola Road, and finally following Viola Road to Mineral.

Mileage Log

0.0 – 7.5   +500,−450 **(15)** Zig-zag west on McGowan Road for 7.5 miles until you reach a **road junction (18)**. Refer to the McGowan Road tour (no. 10) for additional information on this section.

7.5 – 8.8   +300 **(18)** Turn south (left) onto a lesser road and zig-zag southwest on it for 1.3 miles until you reach a **logged area (24)** on the south (left) side of the road. This point is 0.4 mile past the point where the road levels and 100 yards before the road begins to descend.

8.8 – 9.1   +350 **(24)** Climb south, up the logged area, for 0.3 mile until you reach the **ridge line (25)**. On the ridge to the west is a high point. Just east of the high point you will find an excellent perch to view the meadows below.

Eighty-Nine Run **15**

Difficulty	3
Length	1 mile one-way
Elevation	6450/+150,–400 one-way
Navigation	Map (a compass is useful if your sense of direction is poor)
Time	Short
Start	Highway 89, 1.0 mile north of the McGowan Road Trailhead, 3.0 miles north of the junction of Highways 36 and 89, and 2.5 miles south of the Lassen Park Ski Area. There is room to park on the east side of the highway. Additional parking space is located on the east side of the highway and 0.1 mile north. The tour begins on the west side of the road.
End	McGowan Road Trailhead on Highway 89, 2.0 miles north of the junction of Highways 36 and 89, and 3.5 miles south of the Lassen Park Ski Area. There is a turnout, parking space, and the trailhead on the west side of the highway.

You are probably wondering, why put out the effort for a car shuttle in order to ski only one mile? Some people will choose this tour because this very pleasant ski through the woods requires lots of skating turns to negotiate the trees, and because it is all downhill except for the first 0.1 mile. And there is much more.

The tour can be extended to two miles by combining it with the Christie Hill Road tour (no. 9) and to five miles by combining it with the Nancy Creek Road tour (no. 8). These longer tours are well worth the effort required to do the car shuttle.

The Eighty-Nine Run tour begins with a short but steep climb to a flat area. From here a broad ridge, described in the South Approach to Brokeoff Mountain tour (no.16), continues to the northwest and offers excellent touring. Explore the area and practice your downhill techniques on the mild slopes.

Even though this tour is only a mile long and parallels the highway, the dense woods can make navigation difficult. People with a good sense of direction will be able to negotiate it without the aid of a compass. If you lack that sense, if the visibility is poor, or if you prefer the extra safety, you should definitely use a compass. All you need to do is ski south — there are no tricky turns.

15

Mileage Log

0.0 – 0.1 +150 **(26)** Climb west up a steep slope for 0.1 mile to a **level area (27)**. Sometimes the snowbank along the road is high and you will need to look for a good spot to get over it.

0.1 – 1.1 −400 **(27)** Ski south through the trees and parallel to the highway for 1.0 mile until you reach **McGowan Road (28)**. Do not go charging into the trees; ski slowly, look ahead, and search for the path of least resistance. There is a route which avoids all thickets!

1.1 – 1.2 +0 **(28)** Turn east (left) onto McGowan Road and ski 0.1 mile until you reach the **McGowan Road Trailhead (15)**. You will need to turn west (right) onto McGowan Road if you are combining this tour with the Christie Hill Road tour (no. 9) or the Nancy Creek Road tour (no. 8).

Windpacked snow

South Approach to Brokeoff Mountain **16**

Difficulty	2 – 4
Length	Up to 6 miles round trip
Elevation	6450/Up to +1950,–1950 round trip
Navigation	Map (a compass is useful if your sense of direction is poor)
Time	Up to full day
Start	Highway 89, 1.0 mile north of the McGowan Road Trailhead, 3.0 miles north of the junction of Highways 36 and 89, and 2.5 miles south of the Lassen Park Ski Area. There is room to park on the east side of the highway. Additional parking space is located on the east side of the highway and 0.1 mile north. The tour begins on the west side of the road.

You name it, this tour has it: perfect backcountry ski touring terrain, magnificent scenery, and an exhilarating downhill return. Do not be intimidated by the steep slope which you must ascend from the starting point — it is short and a careful, advanced beginner can negotiate it. Your reward for reaching the level area at the top will be some of the best cross-country skiing in the Lassen Volcanic National Park vicinity.

From the level area above the highway a very broad ridge climbs gradually to the northwest. Any skier who can reach the level area will be able to find plenty of interesting touring by following this ridge. The ridge disappears shortly, and the route to the northwest is bordered by dense woods to the west, and dense woods and steep slopes to the east. The amount of land sparsely wooded increases the farther you ski northwest. Although the described route follows a northwest heading which leads to the final steep ascent of Brokeoff Mountain (no. 17) you should feel free to explore at will.

As you ski northwest you will get excellent views of Mt. Conard to the east and glimpses of impressive 9235 foot Brokeoff Mountain, the second highest peak in Lassen Park, to the north. If you get up on the ridge which descends from Brokeoff Mountain you will also have excellent views of Lassen Peak and the forks of Sulphur Creek.

Mileage Log

0.0 – 0.1   +150 **(26)** Climb west up a steep slope for 0.1 mile until you reach a **level area (27)**. Sometimes the snowbank along the road is high and you will need to look for a

16

good spot to get over it.

0.1 – 1.8   +700 **(27)** Ski northwest, at first on a broad ridge, for 1.7 miles to the **Lassen National Forest and Park boundary (29)**. Although the boundary seems like a poor landmark, you can use the boundary signs on the trees to orient yourself in the north-south direction. The terrain becomes noticeably steeper beyond the boundary.

1.8 – 2.6   +700 **(29)** Ski northwest, passing to the west of two knobs, for 0.8 mile until you intersect the **ridge (30)** at a point to the north of the second knob. Be aware that the east side of the ridge is a steep drop and sometimes corniced. Be careful.

2.6 – 3.0   +400 **(30)** Ski north, staying to the west of the ridge, for 0.4 mile until you reach the base of the **steep slope (31)** which leads to the summit of Brokeoff Mountain. The ascent of Brokeoff Mountain is described in the Brokeoff Mountain from the South tour (no. 17). At this location the tour also intersects the Brokeoff Mountain via Forest Lake tour (no. 23).

Brokeoff Mountain from the South **17**

Difficulty	5
Length	7 miles round trip
Elevation	6450/+2800,−2800 round trip
Navigation	Map (a compass is useful if your sense of direction is poor)
Time	Full day
Start	Highway 89, 1.0 mile north of the McGowan Road Trailhead, 3.0 miles north of the junction of Highways 36 and 89, and 2.5 miles south of the Lassen Park Ski Area. There is room to park on the east side of the highway. Additional parking space is located on the east side of the highway and 0.1 mile north. The tour begins on the west side of the road.

Brokeoff Mountain, at 9235 feet, may only be the second highest peak in Lassen Park, but many consider its vertical, brokeoff face as magnificent as monolithic Lassen Peak. The mountain's southwest slope forms a vivid contrast to its vertical face and offers a route for advanced skiers to ascend.

It goes without saying that the views from the summit of Brokeoff Mountain are superb and only surpassed by views from Lassen Peak itself. When you stand on the summit of Brokeoff Mountain you can also look across its face and admire the cornices which overhang. Stay back from the edge.

Although the southwest slope provides a route to the summit, the route can be treacherous when icy and avalanche conditions exist. When conditions are just right, however, the ascent is relatively straightforward and the descent can be a thrilling series of linked turns from the very top. The starting point is 2800 feet below.

If you want to get hooked on the thought of climbing Brokeoff Mountain, take time to admire the mountain as you drive up Highway 89 toward Lassen Park Ski Area. From the road you get an excellent view of both the vertical face and the southwest facing slope along which you ascend the mountain. Brokeoff Mountain Viewpoint on snow-covered Lassen Park Road (no. 24) also affords an impressive view of the mountain's face.

Brokeoff Mountain can also be reached by way of the Brokeoff Mountain via Forest Lake tour (no. 23).

17

Mileage Log

0.0 – 3.0 +1950 **(26)** Ski northwest, climbing continuously, for 3.0 miles until you reach the base of the **steep slope (31)** which leads to the summit of Brokeoff Mountain. Refer to the South Approach to Brokeoff Mountain tour (no. 16) for additional information about this section.

3.0 – 3.5 +850 **(31)** Climb north via the mountain's south ridge and southwest slope for 0.5 mile to the east summit of **Brokeoff Mountain (32)**. Ascend directly up the south ridge until you can turn northwest (left), and climb above a prominent rock outcropping which can be seen from below. Once past the rock outcropping, zig-zag to the summit. A less direct route to the summit follows the general route of the summer hiking trail.

Who is that dashing young skier? Answer on page 55.

Childs Meadows

Childs Meadows is located in a valley east of Morgan Summit (the turnoff on Highway 36 to the Southwest Entrance to Lassen Volcanic National Park). Unfortunately, there are only a few good ski tours in this beautiful area because much of the land is private.

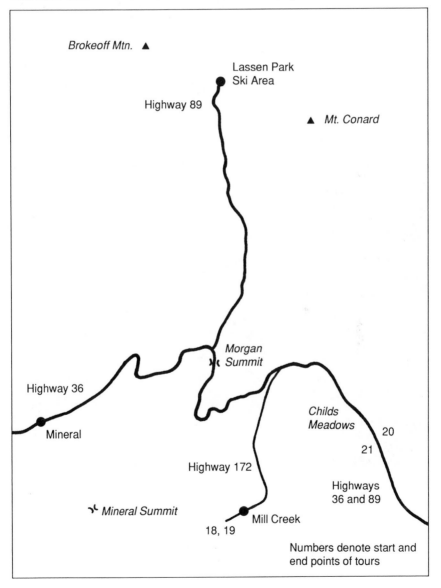

Numbers denote start and end points of tours

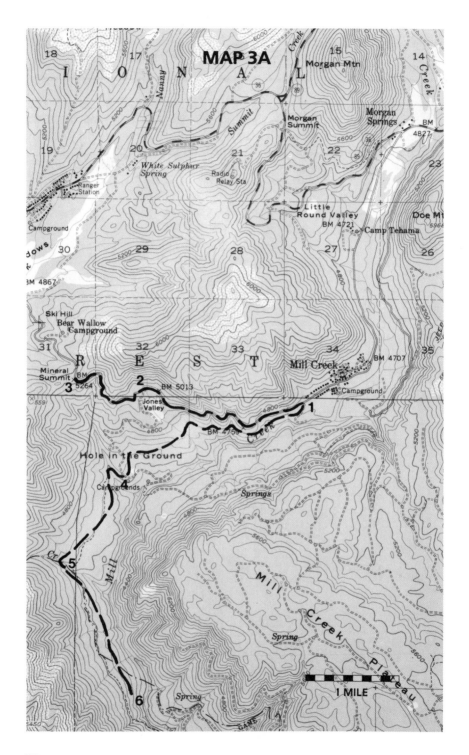

MAP 3A

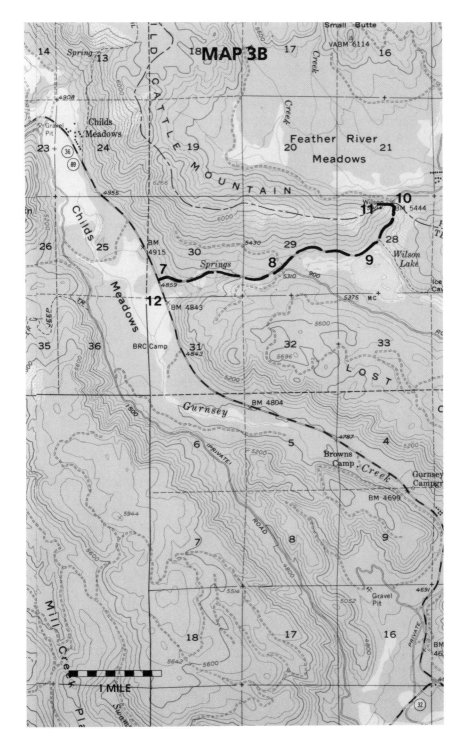

MAP 3B

53

18 Mill Creek to Mineral Summit

MAP 3A
PAGE 52

Difficulty	2
Length	6 miles round trip
Elevation	4600/+650,–650 round trip
Navigation	Road
Time	Half day
Start	End of plowed Highway 172 (Mill Creek Road), 3.4 miles south of Highway 36.

This tour is on an easy-to-follow road which climbs through sheltered terrain to Mineral Summit where the views are unfortunately obscured by the forest. This tour can be combined with the Mineral to Mineral Summit tour (no. 1) to create a one-way tour between Mill Creek and Mineral. Also, a side trip can be made to the meadow at Jones Valley.

Mileage Log

0.0 – 2.0 +450 **(1)** Ski west on Highway 172 for 2.0 miles until you reach the **turnoff to Jones Valley (2)** which is located on the south (left) side of the road. It is 0.4 mile to the meadow at Jones Valley.

2.0 – 3.0 +200 **(2)** Ski west on Highway 172 for 1.0 mile until you reach **Mineral Summit (3)**.

Captian Ski Pole and his good friend Tim

19 Hole In The Ground

Difficulty	1 – 3
Length	Up to 12 miles round trip
Elevation	4600/Up to +700,–700 round trip
Navigation	Road
Time	Up to full day
Start	End of plowed Highway 172 (Mill Creek Road), 3.4 miles south of Highway 36. The tour begins on the Hole In The Ground road which is located on the south (left) side of Highway 172.

The Hole In The Ground tour is a good choice for foul weather days when you are searching for a sheltered tour. It also offers the possibility for a very long tour with little elevation change. At about the half-way point you can also make a side trip to Mill Creek.

The road which this tour follows has so many curves that it would not be possible to get a fair representation of the mileage directly from the topographic map. Therefore, for this tour the mileages were derived by driving the route.

Mileage Log

0.0 – 2.8   +50,–150 **(1)** Ski generally west on the Hole In The Ground road for 2.8 miles until you come to a **road junction (4)**. You can follow the road to the east (left) for 0.6 mile to a summer campground and Mill Creek.

2.8 – 4.5   +150,–100 **(4)** Ski generally southwest (straight) on the Hole In The Ground road for 1.7 miles until you reach **Rock Gulch Creek (5)** where the road makes a relatively sharp turn to the southeast (left).

4.5 – 6.1   –250 **(5)** Ski southeast on the Hole In The Ground road for 1.6 miles until you reach the its **end (6)**.

Wilson Lake **20**

Difficulty	2
Length	5 miles round trip or 6 miles round trip to the saddle beyond the lake
Elevation	4850/+600,−600 round trip or +800,−800 round trip to the saddle beyond the lake
Navigation	Road
Time	Half day
Start	Intersection of Wilson Lake Road and Highway 36, 1.8 miles south of Childs Meadows Resort.

The tour to Wilson Lake makes for a leisurely day of skiing and affords a beautiful setting for lunch. A short extension of the tour will take you to a saddle where a wonderful view of Brokeoff Mountain, Lassen Peak and Mt. Conard awaits.

Mileage Log

0.0 – 1.4   +450 **(7)** Ski east on Wilson Lake Road for 1.4 miles until you reach a **4-way road junction (8)**. As you travel from the highway, you will pass several logging roads and the gradient of the road decreases.

1.4 – 2.3   +50,−100 **(8)** Ski east on Wilson Lake Road for 0.9 mile until you reach **Wilson Lake (9)**.

To continue past Wilson Lake

2.3 – 3.0   +200 **(9)** Ski northeast on Wilson Lake Road for 0.7 mile until you reach a **saddle (10)**. On the other side of the saddle is Feather River Meadows most of which is private property. Also, five roads intersect at the saddle.

3.0 – 3.1   +0 **(10)** Turn onto the road farthest to the left and ski west for 0.1 mile until you get an **open view (11)** of Brokeoff Mountain, Lassen Peak and Mt. Conard.

21 Childs Meadows

Difficulty	1
Length	As desired
Elevation	4850/Nil
Navigation	Adjacent to plowed road
Time	As desired
Start	West side of Highway 36, 2.0 miles south of Childs Meadows Resort and 0.2 mile south of Wilson Lake Road.

Three-mile long Childs Meadows is a series of beautiful meadows in a valley. Since the meadows are private property, most of them are fenced and marked with no trespassing signs. At its south end, however, there is a large section which is neither fenced nor marked, and appears to be open to ski tourers. But, remember that things can change.

The meadows are located on the west side of the highway (12). Ski into the meadows and explore at your leisure.

Lassen Peak

Southwest Entrance

The Southwest Entrance to Lassen Volcanic National Park is the most popular trailhead for cross-country skiing in the park. This entrance provides easy access to the heart of the park's backcountry which includes steaming, bubbling hydrothermal areas, ridges, and peaks. The entrance is located ten miles from Mineral at the Lassen Park Ski Area on Highway 89.

Because the terrain near the Southwest Entrance is generally steep, the most popular ski route is along Lassen Park Road. The steepness also results in avalanche zones near this entrance. Inquire at the Lassen Park Ski Area Ranger Station (First Aid Room) if you are in doubt about the avalanche conditions.

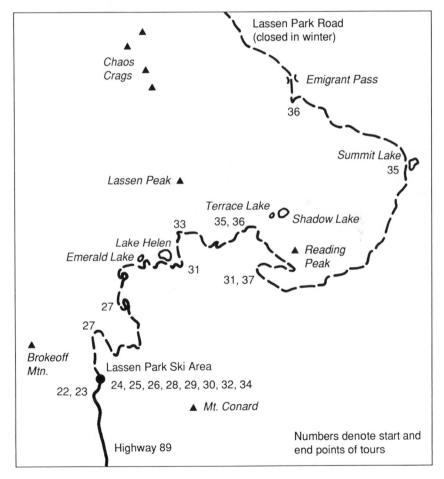

Lassen Park Road
(closed in winter)

Chaos
Crags

Emigrant Pass

36

Summit Lake
35

Lassen Peak ▲

Terrace Lake
33   35, 36   Shadow Lake
Lake Helen
Emerald Lake   ▲ Reading
                31   Peak
                31, 37

27

27

▲
Brokeoff
Mtn.   Lassen Park Ski Area
22, 23   24, 25, 26, 28, 29, 30, 32, 34

                ▲ Mt. Conard

                        Numbers denote start and
                        end points of tours
Highway 89

MAP 4
PAGE 61

22 Forest Lake

Difficulty	4
Length	3 miles round trip
Elevation	6750/+750,–750 round trip
Navigation	Marked trail and map
Time	Half day
Start	The trailhead and sign are located on the west side of the parking area and halfway between the entrance kiosk and the chalet at the Lassen Park Ski Area.

Forest Lake is nestled between dense forest and the steep slopes which form the southeast ridge of Brokeoff Mountain. Although the route to the lake theoretically follows a marked trail you should be aware that the orange markers are sparse, easy to lose track of, and at best should be considered "confidence builders." Since finding the lake is difficult, tourers appear to avoid skiing this interesting tour.

An excellent alternative for the return trip is to retrace your route, at the appropriate spot ski 0.2 mile to the top of the ski area, and then descend the groomed slopes of the ski area. When snow conditions are poor, this route is definitely the best return one.

There is supposed to be a second marked trail to Forest Lake which can be combined with the one described here to make a loop. In reality, I could not follow the second marked trail. All my attempts to return in the general direction of the summer trail ended up in heavy brush.

You can extend the Forest Lake tour to points above the dense forest by continuing toward Brokeoff Mountain as described in the Brokeoff Mountain via Forest Lake tour (no. 23).

Mileage Log

0.0 – 0.2 +50 (1) Ski south and almost parallel to the road for 0.2 mile until you reach the **creek (2)** that drains from springs located east of Forest Lake. The trail does not cross this creek here, however, before reaching this creek you will cross a smaller drainage; do not confuse the drainage with the creek. Beyond this point, the route to Forest Lake heads generally toward Brokeoff Mountain which can occasionally be seen through the trees.

0.2 – 0.4 +100 (2) Ski northwest for 0.2 mile until you reach the

point where the trail crosses the creek (3). Sometimes you will find ski trails from out-of-bounds downhill skiers in this area.

0.4 – 0.7   +200 **(3)** Cross the creek and ski northwest for 0.2 mile until you reach a **clearing (4).** The creek cuts beautiful, deep curves through the clearing.

0.7 – 0.8   +50 **(4)** Ski northwest along the left side of the clearing in order to avoid the creek, and then turn north and climb onto a **ridge (5)** for a total of 0.1 mile. The top of the ski lift is 0.2 mile east of the ridge.

0.8 – 1.1   +200 **(5)** Ski northwest up the ridge while staying slightly on the northeast (right) side of the ridge for 0.2 mile, and then ski west (left) for 0.1 mile until you reach an **open area (6)** which is part of the drainage from the springs located east of Forest Lake.

1.1 – 1.4   +150 **(6)** Ski west for 0.3 mile until you reach **Forest Lake (7).**

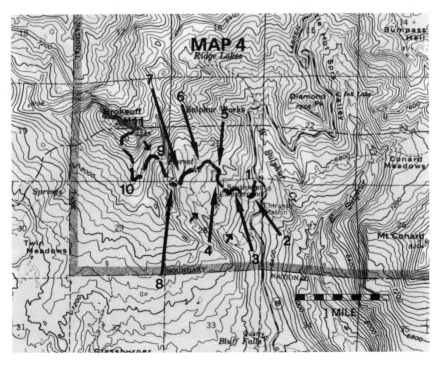

Beautiful, deep curves cut through a clearing

MAP 4
PAGE 61

Brokeoff Mountain
via Forest Lake

23

Difficulty	5
Length	5 miles round trip
Elevation	6750/+2500,–2500 round trip
Navigation	Marked trail and map
Time	Full day
Start	The trailhead and sign are located on the west side of the parking area and halfway between the entrance kiosk and the chalet at the Lassen Park Ski Area.

Two good reasons for making the arduous climb up steep slopes to the summit of Brokeoff Mountain, the park's second highest peak at 9,235 feet, are magnificent views and a thrilling descent.

The tour from the south to Brokeoff Mountain (no. 17) is relatively short and sweet. The tour described here via Forest Lake is even shorter and sweeter — 2500 feet up in only 2.7 miles. An excellent one-way tour is created by ascending via Forest Lake and descending to the south.

Along either route and at the summit you will encounter beautiful but potentially dangerous cornices. Stay well back from their edges. Also be aware that these routes pass through avalanche zones where you must exercise caution. Finally, these routes can be treacherous if icy conditions exist.

Mileage Log

0.0 – 1.3   +750 **(1)** Ski generally northwest for 1.4 miles until you reach **Forest Lake (7)**. Refer to the Forest Lake tour (no. 22) for additional information about this section.

1.4 – 1.5   +50 **(7)** Ski south and then northwest, avoiding the wall on the west side of the lake, for 0.1 mile until you locate a **gully (8)** that heads northwest toward Brokeoff Mountain.

1.5 – 2.0   +600 **(8)** Climb steadily northwest up the gully toward Brokeoff Mountain for 0.5 mile until you reach the steep **southeast face of Brokeoff Mountain (9)**. The terrain opens up as you ascend the gully and these slopes can offer an excellent downhill run on the return trip.

2.0 – 2.3   +250 **(9)** Turn southwest, pass through some trees, and ascend the open slopes for a total of 0.3 mile until you reach the **south ridge (10)** and the steep slope which leads to the summit of Brokeoff Mountain.

2.3 – 2.8   +850 **(10)** Climb north for 0.5 mile to the east summit of **Brokeoff Mountain (11)** via the mountain's south ridge and southwest slope. Ascend directly up the south ridge until you can turn northwest (left), and climb above a prominent rock outcropping which can be seen from below. Once past the rock outcropping, zig-zag to the summit.

Chalet at Lassen Park Ski Area

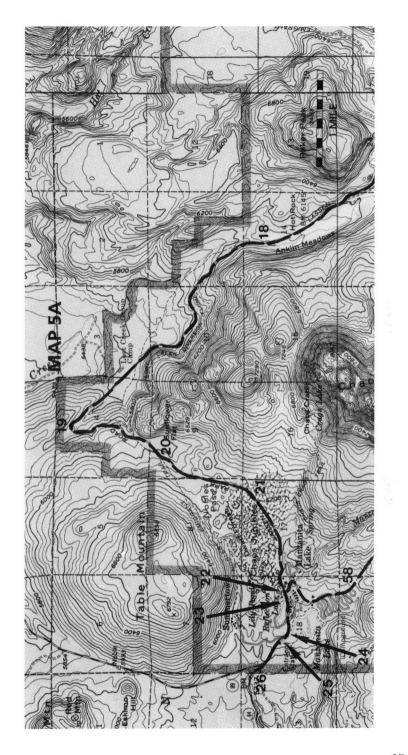

MAP 5A

1 MILE

65

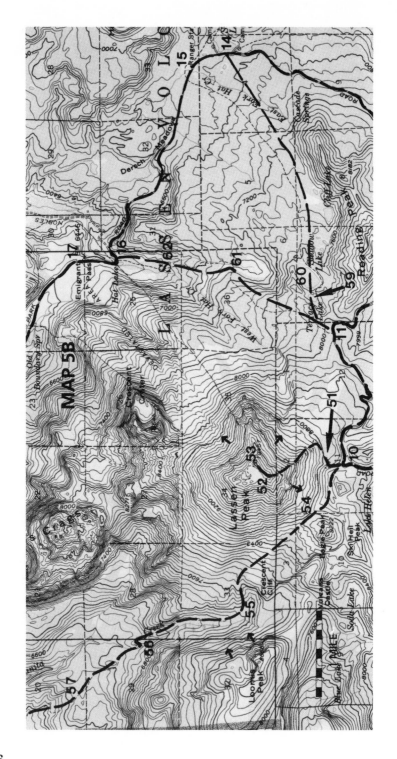

MAP 5B

Lassen Park Road

Lassen Park Road from Lassen Park Ski Area **24**

Difficulty	1 – 5
Length	Up to 29 miles one-way to Manzanita Lake Ranger Station
Elevation	6750/Up to +2350,–3350 one-way to Manzanita Lake Ranger Station
Navigation	Road and map
Time	Few hours to few days
Start	Lassen Park Ski Area chalet where the snow-covered road begins.
End	Same as starting point or the Manzanita Lake Ranger Station on Highway 44.

In winter, snow-covered Lassen Park Road is the main access route to the heart of the park's backcountry. Many skiers visiting the park take day tours along the road; or ski part way on the road, then branch off toward another destination. Other skiers enter the park via the road and spend several days exploring the backcountry. The tour descriptions which follow this one describe many of the destinations which are accessible from the road.

Although unmarked, Lassen Park Road is usually easy to follow except during mid-winter when much of the road between Emerald Lake and Reading Peak vanishes in the open terrain and the large snowpack which normally accumulates at these higher elevations. The terrain off the road is generally steep until you reach Kings Creek eleven miles from the start.

Avalanches present a danger whether you are on or off Lassen Park Road. Of the known avalanche paths which cross the road, some of these are located close to its beginning. Inquire at the Lassen Park Ski Area Ranger Station if you are in doubt about the avalanche conditions. There is also a register for cross-country skiers at the ranger station.

Mileage Log

0.0 – 0.9 +250 (1) Ski north on Lassen Park Road for 0.9 mile until you reach the **bridge (2)** across West Sulphur Creek. The park service asks that you avoid the very first part of the road which passes across the alpine ski slopes by skiing around the chairlift. The bridge is the turnoff point for Ridge Lakes (no. 25).

24

0.9 – 1.0 +0 **(2)** Ski straight on Lassen Park Road for 0.1 mile until you reach the **Sulphur Works (3)**. At the Sulphur Works, an active hydrothermal area, you can hike the short nature trail (boardwalks) located on the north (left) side of the road. The Sulphur Works Cutoff tour (no. 27) also begins here. The cutoff shortens the tour to Emerald Lake and Lake Helen by 1.9 miles and bypasses the portion of Lassen Park Road east of Diamond Peak which is prone to avalanche.

1.0 – 1.7 +100 **(3)** Ski southeast on Lassen Park Road for 0.7 mile until you reach **Brokeoff Mountain Viewpoint (4)**. The viewpoint offers an excellent view to the west of Brokeoff Mountain, the largest remaining part of Mt. Tehama, an 11,000 foot volcano.

1.7 – 2.4 +150 **(4)** Ski east on Lassen Park Road for 0.7 mile until you reach **Diamond Point (5)**. Diamond Point affords a good view to the southeast of the Mill Creek drainage and Mt. Conard.

2.4 – 3.7 +350 **(5)** Ski north on Lassen Park Road for 1.3 miles until you reach **Diamond Peak Saddle (6)**. The saddle is located at the top of an S-turn where the road travels along a ridge-like area. The Sulphur Works Cutoff (no. 27) intersects the road here.

3.7 – 5.3 +500 **(6)** Ski north and east on Lassen Park Road for 1.6 miles until you reach **Emerald Lake (7)**. If you lose sight of the road at Emerald Lake, you can find your way to the east end of Lake Helen where you will be able to pick up the road again. Emerald Lake is the first good snow camping site along Lassen Park Road.

5.3 – 5.9 +100 **(7)** Ski east on Lassen Park Road for 0.6 mile until you reach **Lake Helen (8)**.

5.9 – 6.2 +0 **(8)** Ski east on Lassen Park Road for 0.3 mile until you reach the location where the **road turns north (left) (9)** and begins to climb. The turn in the road is the turnoff point for Bumpass Hell (no. 30) and the start of the Lake Helen Cutoff (no. 31) which shortens the tour on the park road by 3.0 miles.

24

6.2 – 6.8 +300 **(9)** Ski north on Lassen Park Road for 0.6 mile until you reach the flat area which is the **Lassen Peak Trailhead (10)**. The flat area is the start of the steep ascent of Lassen Peak (no. 33) and the Crescent Cliff Traverse (no. 34) intersects Lassen Park Road here.

6.8 – 8.6 −450 **(10)** Ski east on Lassen Park Road for 1.8 miles until you reach the junction with the **Terrace Lake Trailhead (11)** which is located at the base of Reading Peak's west ridge. The trailhead is the turnoff point for the Terrace Lake-Shadow Lake Cutoff (no. 35) and the Paradise Meadow Cutoff (no. 36).

8.6 – 10.9 −600 **(11)**. Zig-zag south on Lassen Park Road for 2.3 miles until you reach the **turnoff to Kings Creek Picnic Area (12)**. Although the road into the picnic area will not be visible, the sign for the turnoff may be. The Lake Helen Cutoff (no. 31) intersects the road here.

10.9 – 11.4 −100 **(12)** Ski southeast on Lassen Park Road for 0.5 mile until you reach **Upper Meadow (13)**.

11.4 – 15.3 −650 **(13)** Ski northeast on Lassen Park Road for 3.9 miles until you reach **Summit Lake (14)**. At this point the Terrace Lake-Shadow Lake Cutoff (no. 35) intersects the road.

15.3 – 15.7 +0 **(14)** Ski north on Lassen Park Road for 0.4 mile until you reach **Summit Lake Ranger Station (15)**. The ranger station is off the road to the northeast (right).

15.7 – 18.1 −250 **(15)** Ski northwest on Lassen Park Road for 2.4 miles until you reach the **West Fork of Hat Creek (16)**. At Hat Creek the Paradise Meadow Cutoff (no. 36) intersects the road. Although Hat Lake is shown on some maps, sedimentation has completely filled it in.

18.1 – 18.5 +0 **(16)** Ski north on Lassen Park Road for 0.4 mile until you reach **Emigrant Pass (17)**.

18.5 – 21.0 −350 **(17)** Ski northwest on Lassen Park Road for 2.5 miles until you reach the location where the road crosses **Lost Creek (18)**.

Sulphur Works Cutoff

21.0 – 24.2 +150,–500 **(18)** Ski northwest on Lassen Park Road for 3.2 miles until you reach the location where the road makes a distinct **sharp (left) turn (19)** and heads south.

24.2 – 25.3 +300 **(19)** Ski southwest on Lassen Park Road for 1.1 miles until you reach the junction with the **Nobles Trail (20)** (no. 39) at Sunflower Flat. The only good landmark for this location is the roadside marker number 60 unless it is covered with snow.

25.3 – 26.4 +150 **(20)** Ski southwest on Lassen Park Road for 1.1 miles until you reach a **high point (21)** on the road.

26.4 – 27.6 –350 **(21)** Ski west on Lassen Park Road for 1.2 miles until you reach the **turnoff to Manzanita Lake Campground (22)** which is on the south (left) side of the road. In this section you will ski past Chaos Jumbles to the south (left) of the road.

27.6 – 27.7 +0 **(22)** Ski west on Lassen Park Road for 0.1 mile until you reach **Reflection Lake (23)** which is on the north (right) side of the road.

27.7 – 28.0 +0 **(23)** Ski west on Lassen Park Road for 0.3 mile until you reach **Manzanita Lake (24)** which is on the south (left) side of the road.

28.0 – 28.1 +0 **(24)** Ski northwest on Lassen Park Road for 0.1 mile until you reach the **Manzanita Lake Entrance Station (25)** and the junction with the Nobles Trail (no. 39).

28.1 – 28.6 –100 **(25)** Ski northwest on Lassen Park Road for 0.5 mile until you reach the **plowed road (26)**. The Manzanita Lake Ranger Station is located 0.1 mile ahead (straight) on the plowed road.

25 Ridge Lakes

Difficulty	4
Length	4 miles round trip
Elevation	6750/+1250,–1250 round trip to lakes or +1550,–1550 round trip via loop
Navigation	Road, marked trail and map
Time	Most of a day
Start	Lassen Park Ski Area chalet where the snow-covered road begins.

After the route to Ridge Lakes leaves Lassen Park Road behind, you find yourself climbing up a beautiful drainage to these secluded lakes and basin. At this perfect lunch spot, the surrounding slopes offer a variety of opportunities for practicing downhill techniques. After your repast, you can make a side trip to the pass 0.3 mile northwest. You should avoid the slopes to the south and southwest of the lakes if avalanche danger exists.

An alternative to retracing your route on the return trip is to ski a loop to the north of Ridge Lakes and beneath the steep slopes of Mt. Diller; do not attempt this route if avalanche danger exists. From the high point of this alternate route the view is great and you descend the first 300 feet in an open bowl.

Mileage Log

0.0 – 0.9   +250 **(1)** Ski north on Lassen Park Road for 0.9 mile until you reach the **bridge (2)** across West Sulphur Creek. The park service asks that you avoid the very first part of the road which passes across the alpine ski slopes by skiing around the chairlift.

0.9 – 1.4   +500 **(2)** Leave the road and ski north (left) up a small, narrow ridge for 0.5 mile until you reach the location where the marked trail crosses a **drainage (27)**. Before you leave the road you should locate the large creek which goes under the bridge. To the east (right) of that creek is a small drainage. To the east (right) of that drainage is the small, narrow ridge which you ascend. Shortly after leaving the road you will reach trees where you should locate the first trail marker. Unfortunately, the trail markers are scarce beyond here.

1.4 – 1.8   +500 **(27)** Cross the drainage, begin to climb and

74

traverse, and follow the marked trail west for 0.5 mile until you reach **Ridge Lakes (28)**.

To complete the loop

1.8 – 2.3   +300 **(28)** Ski to the north end of the lakes and then continue north up a distinct gully for a total of 0.5 mile until you reach the **flat area (29)** just below the steep slopes of Mt. Diller.

2.3 – 2.8   –700 **(29)** Descend the open bowl to the southeast of the flat area and then descend south through trees for a total of 0.5 mile until you intersect the **marked route (30)**. As you approach the marked route you will find the route through the trees very steep.

2.8 – 4.3   –850 **(30)** Retrace your original route for 1.5 miles back to the **ski area (1)**.

Sulphur Works

Lassen Peak

Sulphur Works Loop **26**

Difficulty	2
Length	2 miles round trip
Elevation	6750/+350,–350 round trip
Navigation	Road and map
Time	Few hours
Start	Lassen Park Ski Area chalet where the snow-covered road begins.

The high peaks and steep canyons that make Lassen Volcanic Park's southwest entrance so magnificent also make the ski touring in the area more difficult than elsewhere. Other than skiing on Lassen Park Road, the Sulphur Works Loop tour is the only tour for novice skiers in this area.

From the ski area, this tour follows the Lassen Park Road for one mile to the Sulphur Works; you then return to the ski area by traveling parallel to the park road. You can create a longer tour by skiing farther on the park road and returning via the parallel route.

Be aware that the foot bridge used to cross the West Sulphur Creek on your return is narrow and walking across it may be tricky when it is covered with snow.

Mileage Log

0.0 – 0.9   +250 **(1)** Ski north on Lassen Park Road for 0.9 mile until you reach the **bridge (2)** across West Sulphur Creek (this is not the foot bridge). The park service asks that you avoid the very first part of the road which passes across the alpine ski slopes by skiing around the chairlift.

0.9 – 1.0   +0 **(2)** Ski straight on Lassen Park Road for 0.1 mile until you reach the **Sulphur Works (3)**. The Sulphur Works is an active hydrothermal area, and you can hike the short nature trail (boardwalks) located on the north (left) side of the road.

1.0 – 1.1   +0 **(3)** Ski southeast on Lassen Park Road for 0.1 mile to the **point where you leave the road (31)** on its southwest (right) side; there is no landmark here.

1.1 – 1.9   –350 **(31)** Ski south and parallel to the park road and West Sulphur Creek for 0.8 mile until you reach the

26

foot bridge (32). There is no need to stay close to the creek as you descend through this wide open area. However, when the ski area chalet is almost directly opposite the creek you must move close to the creek and look carefully for the bridge.

1.9 – 2.1   +100 (32) Climb west for 0.2 mile to the ski area **chalet (1)**.

Nature trail at the Sulphur Works

Sulphur Works Cutoff **27**

Difficulty	4
Length	1 mile one-way (saves 1.9 miles)
Elevation	7000/+600 one-way
Navigation	Marked trail
Time	Short
Start	Snow-covered Lassen Park Road at the Sulphur Works which is located 1.0 mile from the Lassen Park Ski Area.
End	Snow-covered Lassen Park Road at Diamond Peak Saddle which is located 3.7 miles from the Lassen Park Ski Area by way of the road. The saddle is located at the top of an S-turn where the road travels along a ridge-like area.

The main feature of the 0.8-mile long Sulphur Works Cutoff is that it can shorten a tour on Lassen Park Road by 1.9 miles. This feature is of particular interest to those skiers who wish to explore points beyond Lake Helen in a single day. In exchange, you must negotiate steeper terrain and navigate without the security of a road.

The Sulphur Works Cutoff can also be used to create a small loop tour and add some variation to an otherwise straightforward tour on Lassen Park Road. In periods of unstable conditions, the cutoff is useful because it bypasses the portion of Lassen Park Road east of Diamond Peak which is prone to avalanche. However, use of the cutoff does not assure complete safety from avalanches.

Although it can be skied in either direction, it is easier to locate the beginning of the marked trail at the Sulphur Works' end. There is a large steam vent on the south (right) side of Lassen Park Road at the Sulphur Works. The cutoff intersects the road just east (beyond) the vent and on the north (left) side of the road. This point is west (before) of the North Fork of West Sulphur Creek.

Mileage Log

0.0 – 0.5   +500 **(3)** Follow the markers north for 0.5 mile until you reach the location where the marked trail crosses the **North Fork of West Sulphur Creek (33)** and turns east (right).

0.5 – 0.8   +100 **(33)** Follow the markers and traverse east for 0.3 mile until you reach **Diamond Peak Saddle (6)**.

28 Brokeoff Mountain Viewpoint Loop

Difficulty	4
Length	3 miles round trip
Elevation	6750/+700,−700 round trip
Navigation	Road, map and compass
Time	Half day
Start	Lassen Park Ski Area chalet where the snow-covered road begins.

This loop presents another opportunity to get off Lassen Park Road and feel the joy of relying on your own backwoods skills. The relatively short descent from the road to the lowest point of the tour offers interesting terrain for the advanced intermediate skier. This tour can be combined with a longer tour on Lassen Park Road.

Mileage Log

0.0 – 1.7 +350 **(1)** Ski north, then southeast on Lassen Park Road for 1.7 miles until you reach **Brokeoff Mountain Viewpoint (4)**. The viewpoint is located at the first turn in the road beyond the Sulphur Works. South of the viewpoint is the ridge around which the tour loops.

1.7 – 1.8 +0 **(4)** Ski north on Lassen Park Road for 0.1 mile until you reach the **clearing (34)** which descends south (right) from the road.

1.8 – 2.3 −700 **(34)** Leave the road and descend south for 0.5 mile until you reach the **south end of a steep ridge (35)**. Most of this descent is through open terrain.

2.3 – 2.7 +250 **(35)** Ski west and then northwest parallel to West Sulphur Creek for 0.4 mile until you reach the **foot bridge (32)** across the creek.

2.7 – 2.9 +100 **(32)** Climb west for 0.2 mile to the ski area **chalet (1)**.

Diamond Peak 29

Difficulty	5
Length	8 miles round trip
Elevation	6750/+1200,−1200 round trip
Navigation	Road and map
Time	Most of a day
Start	Lassen Park Ski Area chalet where the snow-covered road begins.

The summit of Diamond Peak is a spectacular destination. Its small, knife-edged summit gives you a magnificent 360 degree vista, an opportunity to explore the lay-of-the-land from a great height, and the feeling that you are in more remote surroundings.

The first 3.6 miles of the tour to Diamond Peak is along snow-covered Lassen Park Road and the following 0.2 mile off the road is easy too. However, the final and difficult 0.2 mile can be extremely dangerous. The steep terrain, windpacked snow, and icy conditions create hazardous skiing for even expert skiers with metal-edged skis. It is also very important not to attempt the peak when avalanche conditions exist. Nevertheless, Diamond Peak is an extraordinarily fine destination when conditions are just right.

Mileage Log

0.0 – 3.6   +850 **(1)** Zig-zag north on Lassen Park Road for 3.6 miles until you reach the **second turn of an S-turn (36)**. This turn is located 0.1 mile before Diamond Peak Saddle (6).

3.6 – 3.8   +0 **(36)** Leave the road and ski south (left) on a broad ridge for 0.2 mile until the **level terrain abruptly ends (37)**.

3.8 – 4.0   +350 **(37)** Climb south and head for the northwest ridge of Diamond Peak. Cross the ridge and climb to the summit of **Diamond Peak (38)** from its west side.

30 Bumpass Hell

Difficulty	4
Length	14 miles round trip
Elevation	6750/+2050,–2050 round trip
Navigation	Road and map
Time	Full day
Start	Lassen Park Ski Area chalet where the snow-covered road begins.

Bumpass Hell is a basin tightly surrounded by ridges on three sides, and filled with bubbling mud pots, steaming fumaroles, and colorful pools. Since it is Lassen Park's most active hydrothermal area, hundreds of park visitors visit it daily during the summer months. During the winter months, however, you will find the area free of all but the most hardy cross-country skiers.

Although the one-day tour to Bumpass Hell is relatively long, twelve of the miles are on Lassen Park Road. The Sulphur Works Cutoff tour (no. 27) can also be used to reduce the length of the tour by two miles each way. If you are spending a night or two near Lake Helen, the tour to Bumpass Hell becomes a short day tour. Keep in mind that the tour described here does not follow the summer hiking trail; the summer trail is not a good ski route.

Six miles from the start, you leave the security of the road. In the last mile you must ascend a slope which is often icy due to its northern exposure, and then descend a moderately steep slope to Bumpass Hell.

Mileage Log

0.0 – 6.2 +1450 **(1)** Zig-zag north on Lassen Park Road for 6.2 miles until you reach the location east of Lake Helen where the road makes a **turn to the north (left) (9)** and begins to climb. Refer to the Lassen Park Road from Lassen Park Ski Area tour (no. 24) for additional information about this section.

6.2 – 6.4 +200 **(9)** Leave the road and climb east for 0.2 mile until you reach a **low pass (39)**.

6.4 – 6.6 +100 **(39)** Traverse and climb southwest (right) for 0.2 mile until you reach a **plateau (40)**. The route from the pass to the plateau is relatively obvious — it is the most gradual. However, this north-facing slope can get very icy and you should exercise appropriate care to avoid the possibility of a fall which would carry you down to the steeper slopes.

6.6 – 6.9   –100 **(40)** Ski southwest across the plateau for 0.2 mile and then descend southwest for 0.1 mile until you reach a **saddle (41)**. You can see Bumpass Hell before you start the descent if you are close enough to the steep slope which descends directly to it.

6.9 – 7.0   –200 **(41)** Descend east (left) down a steep slope for 0.1 mile until you reach **Bumpass Hell (42)**. Please stay on the boardwalks or snow-covered areas at Bumpass Hell.

Bumpass Hell

31 Lake Helen Cutoff

Difficulty	3
Length	2 miles one-way (saves 3.0 miles)
Elevation	8200/+250,−1000 one-way
Navigation	Map
Time	Short (few hours if skied in reverse direction)
Start	Snow-covered Lassen Park Road at the location east of Lake Helen where the road makes a turn to the north (left) and begins to climb. This location is 6.2 miles from Lassen Park Ski Area by way of the road.
End	Snow-covered Lassen Park Road at the turnoff to Kings Creek Picnic Area which is located 10.9 miles from Lassen Park Ski Area by way of the road.

The Helen Lake Cutoff is an excellent way to reach the heart of Lassen's backcountry in a single day. Skiing the cutoff reduces the tour from the ski area to the Kings Creek Picnic Area to 7.9 miles, a reduction of 3.0 miles. The Kings Creek area offers excellent overnight camping and access to other destinations.

Mileage Log

0.0 – 0.2 +200 **(9)** Leave the road and climb east for 0.2 mile until you reach a **low pass (39)**.

0.2 – 0.7 −300 **(39)** Ski east for 0.5 until you reach the center of a large, open, **flat area (43)**.

0.7 – 1.0 −200 **(43)** Ski northeast for 0.3 mile until you reach **Kings Creek (44)**.

1.0 – 1.7 +50,−500 **(44)** Climb east out of the Kings Creek drainage for 0.1 mile, and then descend southeast and parallel to Kings Creek for 0.6 mile until you reach the **Lassen Park Road (12)** at the turnoff to the Kings Creek Picnic Area. As you descend stay far enough northeast of the creek in order to avoid the worst terrain. When you are 0.2 mile from the end you will encounter a cliff which is best negotiated by skiing closer to the creek. Although the road into the picnic area will not be visible, the sign for the turnoff probably will be.

Conard Lake Loop **32**

Difficulty	5
Length	11 miles round trip
Elevation	6750/+2000,−2000 round trip
Navigation	Road, map and compass
Time	Very long day
Start	Lassen Park Ski Area chalet where the snow-covered road begins.

The Conard Lake Loop covers parts of the Lassen Park Road, Cold Boiling and Crumbaugh Lakes, and Conard Lake and Meadows which are seldom visited in winter. It is a time and energy consuming tour for even hardy skiers. The tour ends with a descent of some of the most difficult terrain described in this guidebook and potentially a very difficult creek crossing. It is a tour for the advanced skier looking for an adventure. If you need to think twice about whether you can do it, you probably should not be doing it.

There are pros and cons for skiing this loop in the direction described here (clockwise) or in the opposite direction (counter-clockwise). I prefer skiing this tour in the clockwise direction. Most of the uphill climb is on Lassen Park Road while the downhill run is in the backcountry. When skiing in this direction, plan to start very early and finish the first 6.2 miles of road travel in three hours or less. The later task of route-finding and other difficulties may take lots of time.

The advantage of skiing this tour in the counter-clockwise direction is that the most difficult sections occur early. If you encounter difficulties and need to retrace your tracks, you have a shorter distance to return. You will also find that in this direction the very, very steep terrain through trees is uphill.

Two challenges of the tour are the steep terrain to the east of East Sulphur Creek and the creek crossing itself. You will find the slopes of the creek drainage too steep to safely descend and ascend in many places. You may also find the creek flow high during the spring, the optimum time for this tour. In this case you will need to search for a snowbridge or rocks on which to cross.

For meeting the challenges of this adventurous tour, you will be rewarded with the pride and satisfaction of accomplishment.

Mileage Log

0.0 – 6.2   +1450 **(1)** Zig-zag north on Lassen Park Road for 6.2 miles until you come to the location east of Lake Helen where the **road turns north (left) (9)** and begins to climb.

6.2 – 6.4 +200 **(9)** Leave the road and climb east for 0.2 mile until you reach a **low pass (39)**.

6.4 – 6.9 –300 **(39)** Ski east for 0.5 mile until you reach the center of a large, open, **flat area (43)**. You will see a small knob at the east end of the flat area.

6.9 – 7.9 –700 **(43)** Ski southeast, pass the small knob to its south (right), descend the southeast ridge of Bumpass Mountain, and finally ski southwest for a total of 1.0 mile until you reach **Cold Boiling Lake (45)**. Depending on your exact route, you may get views of both Cold Boiling and Crumbaugh Lakes as you descend the ridge.

7.9 – 8.6 –150 **(45)** Ski southwest following the Cold Boiling Lake drainage for 0.7 mile until you reach **Crumbaugh Lake (46)**. Do not ski beneath the steep southeast slopes of Bumpass Mountain when avalanche conditions exist.

8.6 – 9.1 +0 **(46)** Ski southwest for 0.5 mile until you reach the very low **saddle (47)** east of Conard Lake.

9.1 – 9.2 –50 **(47)** Ski west for 0.1 mile until you reach **Conard Lake and (Upper) Meadow (48)**.

9.2 – 9.5 –100 **(48)** Ski west through trees for 0.3 mile until you reach **Conard (Lower) Meadow (49)**.

9.5 – 10.2 –700 **(49)** Descend at a very steep angle through very dense woods to the southwest for 0.7 mile until you reach **East Sulphur Creek (50)**. I found a place to cross just above the location where the creek drainage entered a small, but steep canyon.

10.2 – 10.8 +0 **(50)** After crossing the creek and climbing out of the creek drainage, traverse through dense woods for 0.6 mile until you reach the more gradual area at the **south end of a steep ridge (35)**.

10.8 – 11.2 +250 **(35)** Ski west and then northwest parallel to West Sulphur Creek until you reach the **foot bridge (32)**

across the creek.

11.2 – 11.4   +100 **(32)** Climb west for 0.2 mile to the ski area **chalet (1)**.

Bumpass Hell

East Sulphur Creek

Lassen Peak **33**

Difficulty	5
Length	3 miles round trip
Elevation	8500/+1950,−1950 round trip
Navigation	Map
Time	Half day
Start	Snow-covered Lassen Park Road at the Lassen Peak Trailhead which is located 6.8 miles from the Lassen Park Ski Area by way of the road.

At the center of the park stands monolithic Lassen Peak and its 10,457 foot summit which towers above everything else. The peak is relatively young by geologic standards — only 11,000 years — but the snow you ski on hides lava which spewed forth as recently as 1917.

Needless to say, the views from the summit on a clear day are magnificent. You will see north past Mount Shasta into southern Oregon and south to the San Francisco Bay Area.

Since this tour description begins at the Lassen Peak Trailhead, the mileage is very short. From the ski area to the trailhead is 6.8 miles; if you use the Sulphur Works Cutoff (no. 27), you can shorten this route by 1.9 miles. A round trip from the ski area to the summit is a very long and strenuous one-day tour. Many skiers choose to camp at Lake Helen and make the ascent the following morning.

Other skiers wait until the Park Service begins plowing Lassen Park Road from the Southwest Entrance sometime in April. When the road is finally opened in May there is still plenty of snow for a ski ascent of Lassen Peak.

Mileage Log

0.0 – 0.3 +250 **(10)** Climb north for 0.3 mile until you reach an obvious **shelf (51)**. At the shelf you should see the southeast ridge of Lassen Peak along which the summer trail climbs. The ski route follows the same ridge.

0.3 – 1.1 +1700 **(51)** Climb northwest on the ridge for 1.0 mile to the **broad summit area (52)**.

1.1 – 1.3 +0 **(52)** Ski northeast for 0.2 mile to the **summit of Lassen Peak (53)**.

Difficulty	5
Length	14 miles one-way
Elevation	6750/+2050,–3050 one-way
Navigation	Road, marked trail, map and compass
Time	Very long day
Start	Lassen Park Ski Area chalet where the snow-covered road begins.
End	Manzanita Lake Ranger Station on Highway 44. The actual ending point is 0.1 mile before reaching the ranger station where Lassen Park Road is plowed.

A classic tour in Lassen Park is the one-day park crossing from Lassen Park Ski Area in the south to Manzanita Lake in the north via the Crescent Cliff Traverse. The crossing from south to north has a net elevation loss of 1000 feet and is made up of three distinct sections.

The first section is a relatively straightforward 6.8 miles uphill on Lassen Park Road to the Lassen Peak Trailhead. To insure successful completion of this tour, ski this first section early so you have plenty of time to tackle the more difficult remaining sections.

The second section, only 2.0 miles long, is the crux of the tour. Here you must climb to the saddle between Lassen and Eagle Peaks, and then carefully navigate the steep descent around Crescent Cliff to the head of Manzanita Creek.

The third section consists of 5.1 miles downhill on Manzanita Creek Ski Trail and Lassen Park Road to Manzanita Lake Ranger Station. Hit the right snow conditions and this section will be a fitting climax to a spectacular day of touring in this park.

Mileage Log

0.0 – 6.8   +1750 **(1)** Zig-zag north on Lassen Park Road for 6.8 miles until you reach the flat area which is the **Lassen Peak Trailhead (10)**. Refer to the Lassen Park Road from Lassen Park Ski Area tour (no. 24) for additional information about this section.

6.8 – 7.4   +300 **(10)** Leave the road and climb northwest for 0.6 mile until you reach the **saddle (54)** between Lassen and Eagle Peaks. In this section you pass to the north of a small knob and traverse across avalanche prone slopes which descend from Lassen Peak.

34

7.4 – 8.8	–1700 **(54)** Descend northwest for 1.4 miles until you reach the head of **Manzanita Creek (55)**. This is the most critical section of the tour; you must exercise extreme care in avoiding vertical Crescent Cliff. You want to descend the final 0.4 mile to Manzanita Creek on a small ridge located immediately to the north of Crescent Cliff. At Manzanita Creek locate the abandoned Manzanita Lake Fire Road and the marked Manzanita Creek Ski Trail.
8.8 – 10.0	–400 **(55)** Ski north on Manzanita Lake Fire Road and Manzanita Creek Ski Trail for 1.2 miles until you reach the **bridge (56)** across Manzanita Creek.
10.0 – 10.9	–250 **(56)** Ski northwest on Manzanita Lake Fire Road and Manzanita Creek Ski Trail for 0.9 mile until you reach the location where the **road and trail begin to descend (57)**. In this section it is difficult to discern the fire road so it is imperative that you follow the trail markers.
10.9 – 12.0	–550 **(57)** Ski northwest on Manzanita Lake Fire Road and Manzanita Creek Ski Trail for 1.1 miles until you reach the **Manzanita Lake Campground road (58)**. Look carefully for the trail markers where the fire road is not visible.
12.0 – 12.9	–50 **(58)** Ski north on the main campground road for 0.9 mile until you reach **Lassen Park Road (22)**. In this section pass all the campground loops by taking the east (right) fork at all loop road junctions.
12.9 – 13.9	–100 **(22)** Turn west (left) onto and ski on Lassen Park Road for 1.0 mile until you reach the **plowed road (26)**. The Manzanita Lake Ranger Station is located 0.1 mile ahead (straight) on the plowed road.

35 Terrace Lake-Shadow Lake Cutoff

Difficulty	4
Length	3 miles one-way (saves 3.5 miles)
Elevation	8050/–1350 one-way
Navigation	Map and compass
Time	Few hours (half day if skied in reverse direction)
Start	Snow-covered Lassen Park Road at the Terrace Lake Trailhead, 8.6 miles from the Lassen Park Ski Area by way of the road.
End	Snow-covered Lassen Park Road at Summit Lake which is located 15.3 miles from the Lassen Park Ski Area by way of the road.

The Terrace Lake-Shadow Lake Cutoff is a very pleasant tour provided you enjoy skiing in dense woods and do not mind the lack of sun. The tour is over gently sloping terrain except for a couple spots in the vicinity of Terrace Lake and Shadow Lake. If time permits, you can visit Cliff Lake which is nestled up against the steep north face of Reading Peak.

The main feature of the 3.2-mile Terrace Lake-Shadow Lake Cutoff is that it can shorten a tour on Lassen Park Road by 3.5 miles, a hefty savings if you are carrying a heavy pack to your basecamp at Summit Lake. If you are trying to reduce the number of miles on a trans-park tour from the Lassen Park Ski Area to the Manzanita Lake Ranger Station, you may also want to consider the Paradise Meadow Cutoff (no. 36) which cuts off even more miles than this tour. Of course, the skiing and off-road navigation is more difficult than on the road.

Skiers making a basecamp in the backcountry will also find the Terrace Lake-Shadow Lake Cutoff a useful route for creating a loop tour. Create loop tours by combining this route with Lassen Park Road, or by combining it with the Paradise Meadow Cutoff and Lassen Park Road.

The difficulty rating of this tour is based predominantly on the need to navigate with a map and compass through the dense woods which cover the entire distance. Since the tour is all downhill or all uphill, depending on the direction skied, the time necessary to complete it varies greatly.

Mileage Log

0.0 – 0.4   –300 **(11)** Ski north and gradually turn east for 0.4 mile until you reach **Terrace Lake (59)**. You will find a

92

short steep section immediately to the west of the lake which you must descend.

0.4 – 0.6   –100 **(59)** Ski east for 0.2 until you reach **Shadow Lake (60)**. Again you will find a short steep section immediately to the west of the lake which you must descend.

0.6 – 3.2   –950 **(60)** Ski east and gradually turn northeast for 2.6 miles until you reach **Lassen Park Road (14)** at Summit Lake. In this section you will cross the East Fork of Hat Creek. If you do not intersect the road exactly at Summit Lake, you must determine which way to turn in order to reach the lake.

Reading Peak from Lake Helen Cutoff

36 Paradise Meadow Cutoff

MAP 5B
PAGE 66

Difficulty	4
Length	3 miles one-way (saves 7.0 miles)
Elevation	8050/–1600 one-way
Navigation	Map and compass
Time	Few hours (half day if skied in reverse direction)
Start	Snow-covered Lassen Park Road at the Terrace Lake Trailhead, 8.6 miles from the Lassen Park Ski Area by way of the road.
End	Snow-covered Lassen Park Road at the West Fork of Hat Creek which is located 18.1 miles from the Lassen Park Ski Area by way of the road.

The most significant feature of the 2.5-mile Paradise Meadow Cutoff is that it shortens the tour from the Lassen Park Ski Area to the Manzanita Lake Ranger Station via Lassen Park Road by 7.0 miles. If you use this cutoff, the trans-park tour is reduced to 21.6 miles, a reasonable distance for a spring, one-day tour for an expert skier. The Paradise Meadow Cutoff can also be combined with the Terrace Lake-Shadow Lake Cutoff (no. 35) and a section of the Lassen Park Road to make a loop tour.

The difficulty rating of this tour is based predominantly on the need to navigate with a map and compass. Although the Paradise Meadow Cutoff is a steeper descent than the Terrace Lake-Shadow Lake Cutoff, it is less wooded. There are still two obstacles on this route. Just below Paradise Meadow the skiing is made difficult by dense woods and steep terrain. The other obstacle is the need to cross the tributary from Paradise Meadow which enters the West Fork of Hat Creek.

Mileage Log

0.0 – 1.3   –1000 **(11)** Ski slightly east of north for 1.3 miles until you reach the north end of **Paradise Meadow (61)**. You must ski far enough east in order not to miss the meadow, but if you are too far east you will find yourself in steep terrain above Paradise Meadow.

1.3 – 2.0   –600 **(61)** Ski north for 0.7 mile until you reach the location where the Paradise Meadow tributary enters the **West Fork of Hat Creek (62)**. You will need to carefully pick your route in the area just below Paradise

94

36

Meadow. At the junction of the creeks you must find a route across the Paradise Meadow tributary. Do not count on finding a snowbridge.

2.0 – 2.5   +0 **(62)** Ski north on level terrain until you reach **Lassen Park Road (16)** at the bridge across the West Fork of Hat Creek.

Windswept ridge

37 Cold Boiling and Crumbaugh Lakes

Difficulty	2
Length	3 miles round trip
Elevation	7450/+200,–200 round trip
Navigation	Map
Time	Few hours
Start	Snow-covered Lassen Park Road at the turnoff to Kings Creek Picnic Area which is located 10.9 miles from the Lassen Park Ski Area by way of the road.

Skiers visiting the heart of Lassen's backcountry will find the Kings Creek area an excellent place to camp. The possibilities for day tours from this base are countless, limited only by your imagination. Cold Boiling and Crumbaugh Lakes are two possibilities.

You can extend the tour beyond Crumbaugh Lake by continuing to Conard Lake and Meadows as described in the Conard Lake Loop tour (no. 32). The Conard Lake Loop tour also describes an alternate route from Lake Helen to Cold Boiling and Crumbaugh Lakes which is useful to snowcampers doing a day tour from Emerald Lake or Lake Helen.

Mileage Log

0.0 – 0.8 –50 **(12)** Skirt Bumpass Mountain's east ridge by skiing south and then west for a total of 0.8 mile until you reach **Cold Boiling Lake (45)**.

0.8 – 1.5 –150 **(45)** Ski southwest following the Cold Boiling Lake drainage for 0.7 mile until you reach **Crumbaugh Lake (46)**. Do not ski beneath the steep southeast slopes of Bumpass Mountain when avalanche conditions exist.

Manzanita Lake Entrance

The Manzanita Lake Entrance to Lassen Volcanic National Park offers a more tranquil experience than available at the Southwest
Entrance where the ski area is located. On this side of the park you
will find several excellent tours. There is also a short period of time
each winter-spring when it is possible to drive into the Devastated
Area and to ski to places you cannot normally reach in a one-day tour
from either side of the park. Refer to the Devastated Area tour (no.
42) for more information about this feature.

You should also be aware of the reasons for the tranquility and
fewer number of people on the Manzanita Lake side of the park. Near
this entrance there are few overnight accommodations and services,
you will find less snow on this side of the park, and the season is
shorter. Finally, from this entrance you cannot reach the heart of the
park's backcountry in a one-day tour.

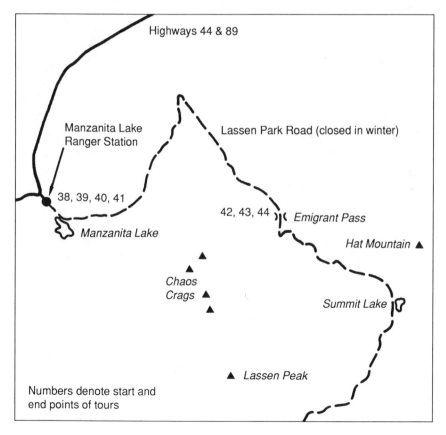

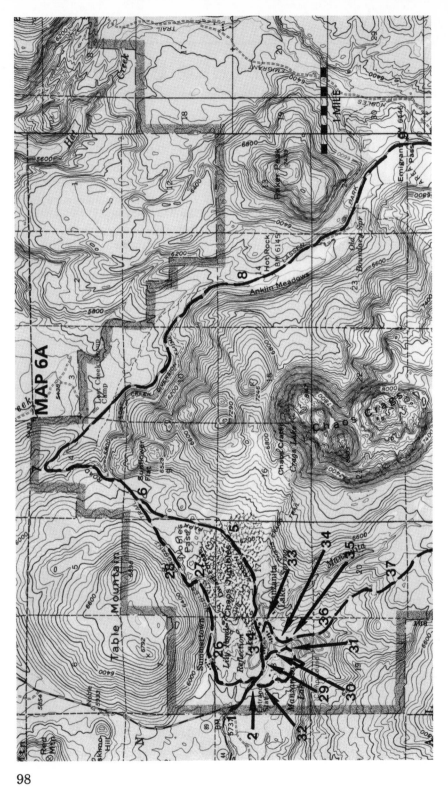

MAP 6A

98

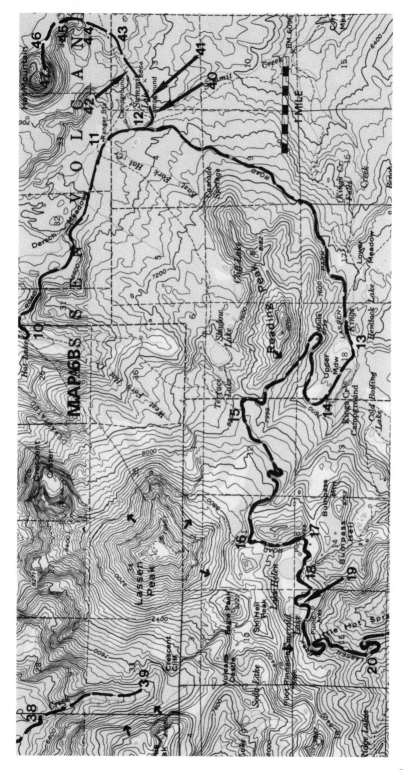

MAP 6B

VOLCANIC

99

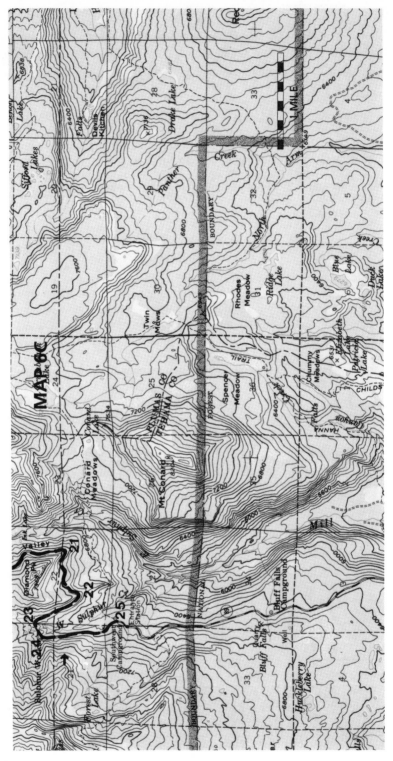

Lassen Park Road from Manzanita Lake Ranger Station   **38**

Difficulty	1 – 5
Length	Up to 29 miles one-way to Lassen Park Ski Area
Elevation	5750/Up to +3350,–2350 one-way to Lassen Park Ski Area
Navigation	Road and map
Time	Few hours to few days
Start	Manzanita Lake Ranger Station on Highway 44. The actual starting point is 0.1 mile beyond the ranger station where Lassen Park Road is not plowed.
End	Same as starting point or the Lassen Park Ski Area.

This tour is a reverse of the Lassen Park Road from Lassen Park Ski Area tour (no. 24). Starting from the Manzanita Lake Ranger Station you will find gentle terrain and fewer skiers than at the ski area end of the road. Also, starting from the Manzanita Lake end there is less avalanche danger on the road unless you are planning to ski beyond Kings Creek (18 miles). Refer to the tour from the ski area (no. 24) for additional information related to the hazards you will encounter beyond Kings Creek.

A ski tour on Lassen Park Road starting from the Manzanita Lake Ranger Station can be a very pleasant experience. After passing Manzanita Lake, Reflection Lake, and Chaos Jumbles at the base of Chaos Crags, you reach a high point 2.2 miles from the start. Beyond the high point the road descends for 1.1 miles to Sunflower Flat and the junction with the Nobles Trail. You can ski a loop by combining a tour on the park road with the Nobles Trail tour (no. 39).

Mileage Log

0.0 – 0.5   +100 **(1)** Ski southeast on Lassen Park Road for 0.5 mile until you reach the **Manzanita Lake Entrance Station (2)**. One hundred feet ahead the Nobles Trail (no. 39) intersects the road on its north (left) side and Manzanita Lake is located on the south (right) side.

0.5 – 0.8   +0 **(2)** Ski southeast on Lassen Park Road for 0.3 mile until you reach **Reflection Lake (3)** which is on the north (left) side of the road.

0.8 – 1.0   +0 **(3)** Ski east on Lassen Park Road for 0.2 mile until you reach the **turnoff to Manzanita Lake Campground (4)** which is on the south (right) side of

101

38

the road. The turnoff is the start of the Manzanita Creek Ski Trail (no. 41) which passes through the campground.

1.0 – 2.2 +350 **(4)** Ski east on Lassen Park Road for 1.2 miles until you reach a **high point (5)** on the road. In this section you will ski past Chaos Jumbles to the south (right) of the road.

2.2 – 3.3 –150 **(5)** Ski northeast on Lassen Park Road for 1.1 miles until you reach the junction with the **Nobles Trail (6)** (no. 39) at Sunflower Flat. The only good landmark for this location is the roadside marker number 60 if it is not covered with snow.

3.3 – 4.4 –300 **(6)** Ski northeast on Lassen Park Road for 1.1 miles until you reach the location where the road makes a distinct **sharp (right) turn (7)** and heads southeast.

4.4 – 7.6 +500,–150 **(7)** Ski southeast on Lassen Park Road for 3.2 miles until you reach **Lost Creek (8)**.

7.6 – 10.1 +350 **(8)** Ski southeast on Lassen Park Road for 2.5 miles until you reach **Emigrant Pass (9)**.

10.1 – 10.5 +0 **(9)** Ski south on Lassen Park Road for 0.4 mile until you reach the **West Fork Hat Creek (10)**. At Hat Creek the Paradise Meadow Cutoff tour (no. 36) intersects the road. Although Hat Lake is shown on some maps, sedimentation has completely filled it in.

10.5 – 12.9 +250 **(10)** Ski southeast on Lassen Park Road for 2.4 miles until you reach **Summit Lake Ranger Station (11)**. The ranger station is off the road to the northeast (left).

12.9 – 13.2 +0 **(11)** Ski south on Lassen Park Road for 0.3 mile until you reach **Summit Lake (12)**. At this point the Terrace Lake-Shadow Lake Cutoff tour (no. 35) intersects the road.

13.2 – 17.0 +650 **(12)** Ski southwest on Lassen Park Road for 3.8 miles until you reach **Upper Meadow (13)**.

17.0 – 17.7 +100 **(13)** Ski northwest on Lassen Park Road for 0.7 mile until you reach the turnoff to **Kings Creek Picnic**

Fresh snow on Lassen Park Road

38

Area **(14)**. Although the road into the picnic area will not be visible, the sign for the turnoff may be. If you take the Lake Helen Cutoff (no. 31) which intersects the road here, you shorten the tour on the park road by 3.0 miles.

17.7 – 20.0 +600 **(14)** Zig-zag north on Lassen Park Road for 2.3 miles until you reach the **Terrace Lake Trailhead (15)** which is located at the base of Reading Peak's west ridge. The trailhead is the turnoff point for the Terrace Lake-Shadow Lake Cutoff tour (no. 35) and the Paradise Meadow Cutoff tour (no. 36).

20.0 – 21.8 +450 **(15)** Ski west on Lassen Park Road for 1.8 miles until your reach the flat area which is the **Lassen Peak Trailhead (16)**. The flat area is the start of the steep ascent of Lassen Peak (no. 33) and the Crescent Cliff Traverse (no. 34) intersects Lassen Park Road here.

21.8 – 22.4 –300 **(16)** Ski south on Lassen Park Road for 0.6 mile until you reach the location where the **road turns west (right) (17)** and levels off. The Lake Helen Cutoff (no. 31) intersects the road here.

22.4 – 22.7 +0 **(17)** Ski west on Lassen Park Road for 0.3 mile until you reach **Lake Helen (18)**. You may lose sight of the road at Lake Helen, but it is not difficult to find your way to Emerald Lake.

22.7 – 23.3 –100 **(18)** Ski west on Lassen Park Road for 0.6 mile until you reach **Emerald Lake (19)**. If you have not been following the road, you will be able to find it again approximately 0.1 mile west of Emerald Lake.

23.3 – 24.9 –500 **(19)** Ski west and south on Lassen Park Road for 1.6 miles until you reach **Diamond Peak Saddle (20)**. The saddle is located at the top of an S-turn where the road travels along a ridge-like area. The Sulphur Works Cutoff tour (no. 27), which shortens the tour by 1.9 miles, leaves the road at this point. It bypasses the portion of Lassen Park Road east of Diamond Peak that is prone to avalanche.

24.9 – 26.2 –350 **(20)** Ski south on Lassen Park Road for 1.3 miles until you reach **Diamond Point (21)**. Diamond Point offers a good view to the southeast of the Mill Creek drainage and Mt. Conard.

26.2 – 26.9   –150 **(21)** Ski west on Lassen Park Road for 0.7 mile until you reach **Brokeoff Mountain Viewpoint (22)**. The viewpoint offers an excellent view to the west of Brokeoff Mountain, the largest remaining part of Mt. Tehama, an 11,000 foot volcano.

26.9 – 27.6   –100 **(22)** Ski northwest on Lassen Park Road for 0.7 mile until you reach the **Sulphur Works (23)**. At the Sulphur Works, an active hydrothermal area, you can hike the short nature trail (boardwalks) located on the north (right) side of the road. The Sulphur Works Cutoff tour (no. 27) intersects the road here.

27.6 – 27.7   +0 **(23)** Ski straight on Lassen Park Road for 0.1 mile until you reach the **bridge (24)** across West Sulphur Creek.

27.7 – 28.6   –250 **(24)** Ski south on Lassen Park Road for 0.9 mile until you reach **Lassen Park Ski Area** (25).

Crescent Cliff

Nobles Trail **39**

Difficulty	3
Length	7 miles round trip
Elevation	5750/+650,–650 round trip
Navigation	Road and marked trail
Time	Most of a day
Start	Manzanita Lake Ranger Station on Highway 44. The actual starting point is 0.1 mile beyond the ranger station where Lassen Park Road is not plowed.

William Nobles, a prospector, discovered the Nobles Trail in 1851 where a road was constructed a year later. Until the completion of the Transcontinental Railroad in 1869, this was the best route across northeastern California to the Upper Sacramento Valley.

Today, the historic Nobles Trail, sometimes referred to as the Emigrant Trail, makes a good loop tour when combined with part of Lassen Park Road. The Nobles Trail section of the tour climbs 400 feet along the southeast flank of Table Mountain before it descends through heavy timber to the park road at Sunflower Flat.

As you ski on Lassen Park Road, you will have great difficulty in spotting the Nobles Trail at Sunflower Flat unless the roadside marker number 60 is visible. Therefore, to make the loop first ski the Nobles Trail, marked with brightly colored triangles, and return via the park road.

Mileage Log

0.0 – 0.5   +100 **(1)** Ski southeast on Lassen Park Road for 0.5 mile until you reach the **Manzanita Lake Entrance Station (2)**. One hundred feet ahead the Nobles Trail intersects the road on its north (left) side and Manzanita Lake is located on the south (right) side.

0.5 – 1.2   +0 **(2)** Turn north (left) onto the Nobles Trail and follow the road for 0.7 mile until you reach the **end of the road (26)**. Here you will find powerlines crossing the road and you will find a small building if it has not yet been torn down.

1.2 – 2.1   +250 **(26)** Climb gradually east on the marked trail for 0.9 mile until you reach the point where the **trail turns north (27)**.

107

39

2.1 – 2.5   +150 **(27)** Climb north and northeast on the marked trail for 0.4 mile until you reach **Nobles Pass (28).** Nobles Pass is actually 50 feet higher than the gap 200 yards to the south.

2.5 – 3.4   –200 **(28)** Descend northeast on the marked trail through a narrow cut in the heavy timber for 0.9 mile until you reach Lassen Park Road at **Sunflower Flat (6).**

3.4 – 4.5   +150 **(6)** Turn southwest (right) onto Lassen Park Road and ski for 1.1 miles until you reach a **high point (5)** on the road.

4.5 – 5.7   –350 **(5)** Ski west on Lassen Park Road for 1.2 miles until you reach the **turnoff to Manzanita Lake Campground (4)** which is on the south (left) side of the road. In this section you will ski past Chaos Jumbles to the south (left) of the road.

5.7 – 5.8   +0 **(4)** Ski west on Lassen Park Road for 0.1 mile until you reach **Reflection Lake (3)** which is on the north (right) side of the road.

5.8 – 5.9   +0 **(3)** Ski west on Lassen Park Road for 0.3 mile until you reach **Manzanita Lake (29)** which is on the south (left) side of the road.

5.9 – 6.2   +0 **(29)** Ski northwest on Lassen Park Road for 0.1 mile until you reach the **Manzanita Lake Entrance Station (2).**

6.2 – 6.7   –100 **(2)** Ski northwest on Lassen Park Road for 0.5 mile until you reach the **plowed road (1).**

Lassen Peak from West Fork Hat Creek

40 Manzanita Lake

Difficulty	2
Length	2 to 3 miles round trip
Elevation	5750/Up to +100,−100 round trip
Navigation	Road and map
Time	Few hours
Start	Manzanita Lake Ranger Station on Highway 44. The actual starting point is 0.1 mile beyond the ranger station where Lassen Park Road is not plowed.

The nearly flat tour around Manzanita Lake would be ideal for first time skiers except for places along the route where you must pass through dense trees. First time skiers will probably prefer to ski on Lassen Park Road (no. 38) or on the Manzanita Creek Ski Trail (no. 41) which passes through the campground. The Manzanita Creek Ski Trail tour also describes how to combine a tour through the campground with the ski around the lake.

Mileage Log

0.0 – 0.5   +100 **(1)** Ski southeast on Lassen Park Road for 0.5 mile until you reach the **Manzanita Lake Entrance Station (2)**. Manzanita Lake is 100 feet ahead on the south (right) side of the road.

0.5 – 0.7   +0 **(2)** Ski southeast on Lassen Park Road for 0.2 mile until the **road begins to leave the lake shore (29)**.

0.7 – 0.9   +0 **(29)** Leave Lassen Park Road on its south (right) side and ski around Manzanita Lake until you reach the **bridge (30)** across the inlet to the lake. Note that the bridge is located 0.1 mile from the lake where the summer hiking trail crosses the inlet.

0.9 – 1.0   +0 **(30)** Ski south for 0.1 mile until you reach a **summer parking area (31)**. This is the location at which you can pick up the Manzanita Lake tour if you are skiing the Manzanita Creek Ski Trail.

1.0 – 1.9   +0 **(31)** Ski around Manzanita Lake for 0.9 mile until you reach the **outlet of the lake (32)**. The bridge across the outlet is located at the edge of the lake.

1.9 – 2.0   +0 **(32)** Ski north for 0.1 mile until you reach the **Man-**

zanita Lake Entrance Station (2).

2.0 – 2.5   –100 **(2)** Ski northwest on Lassen Park Road for 0.5 mile until you reach the **plowed road (1)**.

Ice covered trees

41 Manzanita Creek Ski Trail

Difficulty	1 – 3
Length	Up to 5 miles one-way to the base of Crescent Cliff
Elevation	5750/Up to +1350 one-way to the base of Crescent Cliff
Navigation	Road, marked trail and map
Time	Up to full day
Start	Manzanita Lake Ranger Station on Highway 44. The actual starting point is 0.1 mile beyond the ranger station where Lassen Park Road is not plowed.

Away from the main road, Manzanita Creek Ski Trail allows you to enjoy the feeling of being in the backwoods alone and away from the trappings of man. You will have a close-up view of Lassen and Loomis Peaks at the mid-point of the tour, and a view of the sheer walls of Crescent Cliff at the far point of the tour, but they will not be panoramic views.

The first two miles of the tour to the far end of Manzanita Lake Campground are very easy and suitable for first time skiers. Once you reach the campground you have four alternatives: continue on the Manzanita Creek Ski Trail, ski around in the campground, ski around Manzanita Lake, or return via the same route you already skied.

Beyond the campground Manzanita Creek Ski Trail climbs 1200 feet on abandoned Manzanita Lake Fire Road to the base of Crescent Cliff. The climb is divided into two distinct sections — the first section climbs 600 feet in one mile; the second section climbs 600 feet in two miles. Between the two sections is a distinct level area which makes a good intermediate destination or rest stop.

Snow campers will find good sites along the upper section of Manzanita Creek Ski Trail where running water can be found. However, be aware that it is not safe to camp, or for that matter ski, in some areas close to Loomis Peak. For current conditions consult the park ranger.

The Manzanita Creek Ski Trail is also part of the Crescent Cliff Traverse (no. 34) which is the shortest ski route between the Manzanita Lake and Southwest Entrances to the park.

Mileage Log

0.0 – 1.0 +100 **(1)** Ski southeast and east on Lassen Park Road for 1.0 mile, past the Manzanita Lake Entrance Station, and Manzanita and Reflection Lakes, until you reach the **turnoff to Manzanita Lake Campground (4)** which is on the south (right) side of the road. You can see Lassen Peak and Loomis Peak from the turnoff. Refer to the Lassen Park Road from Manzanita Lake Ranger Station tour (no. 38) for additional information about this section.

1.0 – 1.2   +0 **(4)** Turn south (right) onto the the Manzanita Lake Campground road and loop south for 0.2 mile until you reach **Manzanita Creek (33)**. Fifty feet before reaching the creek you pass the Chaos Crags summer hiking trail on the east (left) side of the road.

1.2 – 1.4   +0 **(33)** Ski southwest (straight) on the Manzanita Lake Campground road for 0.2 mile until you reach an **access point for Manzanita Lake (34)** on the west (right) side of the road. This access point is the easiest to the lake if you desire to return to the Manzanita Lake Entrance Station by skiing around the lake. The summer parking area referred to in the Manzanita Lake tour (no. 40) is located a very short distance to the west of this access point.

1.4 – 1.5   +0 **(34)** Ski south (straight) on the Manzanita Lake Campground road for 0.1 mile until you reach the summer **camper services buildings (35)**.

1.5 – 1.9   +50 **(35)** Ski south (straight) on the main campground road for 0.4 mile until you reach the start of abandoned **Manzanita Lake Fire Road (36)** (Manzanita Creek Ski Trail). In this section you will encounter campground Loops C through F (loops A and B shown on the topographic map do not exist); always take the east (straight) fork. The fire road and ski trail leave the campground road 25 feet past the start of campground Loop F.

1.9 – 3.0   +550 **(36)** Ski southeast on Manzanita Lake Fire Road and Manzanita Creek Ski Trail for 1.1 miles until you reach the location where the **road and ski trail distinctly level (37)**. Since snow can easily obscure the fire road, locate the trail markers to guide you. The trail markers are a combination of brightly colored triangles

Creek crossing

and circles. When you reach the level area you are 3.0 miles from the start of the tour. Directly in front of you to the southeast is Lassen Peak and to the south is Loomis Peak. Manzanita Creek Ski Trail continues up the Manzanita Creek drainage which descends from between Lassen Peak and Loomis Peak.

3.0 – 3.9   +250 (37) Ski southeast on Manzanita Lake Fire Road and Manzanita Creek Ski Trail for 0.9 mile until you reach the **bridge (38)** across Manzanita Creek. In this section it is difficult to discern the fire road so it is imperative that you follow the trail markers. If in doubt, remember that the trail heads up the drainage between Lassen Peak and Loomis Peak which means that you will need to veer slightly south (right).

3.9 – 5.1   +400 (38) Ski south on abandoned Manzanita Lake Fire Road and Manzanita Creek Ski Trail for 1.2 miles until you reach the **head of the canyon (39)** and the headwaters of Manzanita Creek. At the head of the canyon you will see the sheer walls of Crescent Cliff above.

42 Devastated Area

Difficulty	1 – 5
Length	As desired
Elevation	6450/Elevation change depends on route chosen
Navigation	Road, map, and/or compass
Time	Short to full day
Start	Lassen Park Road near Emigrant Pass, 10.1 miles southeast of the Manzanita Lake Ranger Station. This location can be reached only from the Manzanita Lake Entrance to the park. Details concerning access to this point are given in the description below.

Ski tours beginning from the Devastated Area (9) offer easy access to the heart of Lassen Park's backcountry and afford an opportunity to explore and enjoy the beauty and solitude of the area. The Devastated Area is only accessible by vehicle for a short time during the ski season, but the opportunities it affords make the planning well worth the effort.

Throughout the winter months access to these backcountry areas require many miles of skiing beginning from either the Lassen Park Ski Area or Manzanita Lake Ranger Station. Even an accomplished skier would find a one-day tour into these areas long with no time left for exploration. During this season snowcamping is the only way to immerse oneself in the delights of these areas.

The onset of spring, however, brings with it a different picture. Many feet of snow may still cover Lassen Park Road at the Lassen Park Ski Area (southwest) end, but the smaller accumulation of snow on the road at the Manzanita Lake Ranger Station (north) end disappears much earlier. When the snow conditions for cross-country skiing become marginal at the north end, the National Park Service plows the park road to the Devastated Area thereby creating the perfect starting point for cross-country skiers interested in venturing into the backcountry. Good conditions for skiing last for another month or so.

The date the plowing begins depends on the snowpack. In general, the plowing begins in late March or early April. Before making a long trip, contact the park service to verify that the road to the Devastated Area is open. Unfortunately, no camping is permitted at the trailhead. In some years the Manzanita Lake Campground is open for car camping at about the same time the road is plowed.

Skiers of all abilities will find excellent touring opportunities beginning at the Devastated Area. Beginners can explore the easy terrain in the vicinity of the parking area or ski on the snow-covered road. The very level 3.0 miles on the road to Summit Lake is a popular choice.

The opening of the road to the Devastated Area makes day tours into the backcountry beyond Summit Lake reasonable for intermediate skiers. This area is filled with perfect terrain for touring, and magnificent vistas of monolithic Lassen Peak, the cliffs of Reading Peak, and the park backcountry to the east and north. The Beyond Summit Lake tour (no. 43) describes one alternative.

Once the Devastated Area becomes accessible by vehicle, only 18.4 miles of Lassen Park Road remains snow-covered. With longer spring days, route-finding on the road, and firm snow, the trans-park tour on the road becomes a reasonable objective for more skiers. If you have two groups of skiers, one beginning from each end, you can swap keys in the middle of this tour thereby simplifying the logistics. Refer to the Lassen Park Road tours (nos. 24 and 38) for more information.

More advanced skiers can explore the flanks of Lassen Peak. A very interesting tour can be created by combining the Terrace Lake-Shadow Lake Cutoff (no. 35), the Paradise Meadow Cutoff (no. 36), and the park road into a loop. This loop takes you up near the steep cliffs of Reading Peak. When planning this tour, be aware that you may have to get wet to cross the West Fork of Hat Creek.

Easy skiing

Beyond Summit Lake **43**

Difficulty	3
Length	10 miles round trip to third plateau. Many other options exist.
Elevation	6450/+900,–900 round trip to third plateau
Navigation	Road and map (compass may be useful)
Time	Most of a day. Longer options exist.
Start	Lassen Park Road near Emigrant Pass, 10.1 miles southeast of the Manzanita Lake Ranger Station. This location can be reached only from the Manzanita Lake Entrance to the park. Details concerning access to this point are given in the Devastated Area tour (no. 42).

A one-day tour into the backcountry beyond Summit Lake is a treat afforded by vehicle access to the Devastated Area (no. 42). Once you arrive at Summit Lake (3.0 miles on Lassen Park Road) you are faced with the choice of which direction to ski into the backcountry. Your options for tours are only limited by your imagination.

This tour describes a route to the northeast of Summit Lake which is a succession of short climbs separated by plateaus. More and more of the Lassen backcountry becomes visible as you climb above the lake. As you climb, the magnificent views of Lassen Peak and Reading Peak previously hidden by the forest appear.

By the time you reach the top of the third plateau, you will have a much better prospective of the excellent touring terrain which exists in this backcountry area. To the north, east, and south there are miles of intermediate touring terrain filled with lakes and cinder cones. Some of these places may require a multi-day tour to explore.

Although Lassen Peak and Reading Peak are obvious landmarks to guide you back to Lassen Park Road, there are limited landmarks to follow from the road to the third plateau. If you are unsure of your navigation with map only, you may desire the aid of a compass. It can be especially useful in crossing the wooded plateaus.

The vastness of the excellent touring terrain in this area makes possible numerous variations of the described route. Use your own judgment. The Hat Mountain tour (no. 44) is an extension of the tour described here.

Mileage Log

0.0 – 0.4   +0 **(9)** Ski south on Lassen Park Road for 0.4 mile until

43

you reach the **West Fork Hat Creek (10)**.

0.4 – 2.8   +250 **(10)** Ski southeast on Lassen Park Road for 2.4 miles until you reach the **Summit Lake Ranger Station (11)**. The ranger station is off the road to the northeast (left).

2.8 – 3.1   +0 **(11)** Ski south on Lassen Park Road for 0.3 mile until you reach **Summit Lake (12)** and the entrance to the north campground.

3.1 – 3.4   +0 **(12)** Ski south along the west side of Summit Lake for 0.3 mile until you reach its **outlet (40)** and cross to its east side. This is the starting point of the climb to the first plateau.

3.4 – 3.6   +150 **(40)** Climb east for 0.2 mile until you reach the **first plateau (41)**.

3.6 – 3.9   +0 **(41)** Ski northeast across the first plateau for 0.3 mile until you reach the **starting point of the climb to the second plateau (42)**.

3.9 – 4.2   +300 **(42)** Climb northeast for 0.3 mile until you reach the **second plateau (43)**.

4.2 – 4.6   +0 **(43)** Ski northeast across the second plateau for 0.4 mile until you reach the **starting point of the climb to the third plateau (44)**.

4.6 – 4.8   +150 **(44)** Climb north for 0.2 mile until you reach the **third plateau (45)**.

4.8 – 5.2   +50 **(45)** Ski northwest along the edge of the plateau for 0.4 mile until you reach the start of the **steep ridge (46)** that ascends Hat Mountain.

Hat Mountain **44**

Difficulty	4
Length	11 miles round trip
Elevation	6450/+1250,–1250 round trip
Navigation	Road and map (compass may be useful)
Time	Most of a day
Start	Lassen Park Road near Emigrant Pass, 10.1 miles southeast of the Manzanita Lake Ranger Station. This location can be reached only from the Manzanita Lake Entrance to the park. Details concerning access to this point are given in the Devastated Area tour (no. 42).

Hat Mountain dominates the view to the east from the parking area. Although the mountain has the shape of a cinder cone, it is actually the result of large lava flows.

The ascent of Hat Mountain is a short extension of the Beyond Summit Lake tour (no. 43). As you would expect, the vistas from the summit are the highlight of the ascent. The final 0.3 mile of the tour ascends a steep, narrow ridge to the high point on the south rim of the crater.

Mileage Log

0.0 – 5.2   +900 **(9)** Follow the Beyond Summit Lake tour (no. 43) for 5.2 miles until you reach the **steep ridge (46)** that ascends Hat Mountain.

5.2 – 5.5   +350 **(46)** Climb west up the steep, narrow ridge that ascends to the **south rim of the crater (47)**. The dense woods in the gully to the north (right) of the ridge make the gully a poor alternative.

Are we having fun yet?

Rentals and Instruction

The following locations offer cross-country ski rental equipment and instruction. It is recommended that you determine their days and hours of operation prior to arriving.

Mineral Lodge Sport Shop
Center of Mineral
Offers cross-country ski rental equipment
916-595-4422

Lassen Park Ski Area
Southwest Entrance to the park
Offers cross-country ski rental equipment
and lessons including telemark lessons
916-595-3376

Fire Mountain Lodge
15 miles east of Mineral on Highway 36
Offers cross-country ski rental equipment
916-258-2938

Lodging

The following locations offer lodging, food services and store goods. It is recommended that you determine their days and hours of operation prior to arriving.

Mineral Lodge
Lodging, restaurant, and store
Center of Mineral
916-595-4422

McGoverns' Vacation Chalets
Cabin rentals
Mineral
415-897-8377

Childs Meadows Resort
Lodging and cafe
9 miles east of Mineral on Highway 36
916-595-4411

Mill Creek Resort
Lodging, cafe, and store
3 miles south of Highway 36
on Highway 172 (Mill Creek Road)
916-595-4449

Fire Mountain Lodge
Lodging, cafe, and store
15 miles east of Mineral on Highway 36
916-258-2938

Deer Creek Lodge
Lodging and cafe
19 miles east of Mineral on Highway 36
916-258-2939

Black Forest Lodge
Lodging and restaurant
20 miles east of Mineral on Highway 36
916-258-2941

St. Bernard Lodge
Lodging and restaurant
20 miles east of Mineral on Highway 36
916-258-3382

Hat Creek Resort
Lodging, pizza and sandwich shop, and store
11 miles north of the Manzanita Lake
Ranger Station on Highway 44
916-335-7121

Help and Information

To Report An Emergency
Lassen Volcanic National Park Headquarters
916-595-4444
Manzanita Lake Ranger Station
916-335-7373
or dial 911

Backcountry Information
Lassen Park Ski Area
First Aid Room
916-595-3308
Manzanita Lake Ranger Station
916-335-7373

Parkcast
Weather forecasting for
Western Regional National Parks
415-556-6030

Road Conditions
916-244-1500 or 415-654-9890

Nordic Voice

The *Nordic Voice* is published by backcountry skiers seeking to protect the aesthetic qualities of wilderness and the future of the sport they love. You can stay informed of the issues affecting Nordic skiers by sending for your *free* subscription.

To promote the interests of Nordic skiers in California

To preserve and protect existing
backcountry winter recreation areas

To encourage and promote opportunities
for the winter wilderness experience

Nordic Voice
c/o Bittersweet Publishing Company
P.O. Box 1211
Livermore, California 94550